EUROPE
By Van and Motorhome

David Shore
and
Patty Campbell

Other books by David Shore and Patty Campbell:

Europe Free! The Car, Van & RV Travel Guide
New Zealand by Motorhome
Patty's On-the-Road Gourmet

Direct all orders to:

Shore/Campbell Publications
1842 Santa Margarita Drive
Fallbrook, California 92028
Telephone (619) 723-6184

Cover photo: Patty Campbell in motorhome at Neuschwanstein Castle, Germany, by David Shore. Rimor/Ford motorhome from Braitman & Woudenberg, Amsterdam.

Motorhome illustrations and diagrams by permission of Braitman & Woudenberg, Eliza Travel, Global Motorhome Travel, and Reisebüro Marti.

Printed on recycled paper.

The paper in this book meets the ANSI Standard Z39.48-1984
for permanence of paper for printed library material.

EUROPE
By Van
and Motorhome

David Shore and Patty Campbell

Shore/Campbell Publications

Fallbrook, California

Library of Congress Catalog Card Number: 94-92022

ISBN 0-938297-08-2 (pbk.) $13.95

This book is as complete and accurate as possible. Facts
have been exhaustively checked and rechecked, based
upon authoritative information available at the time of
printing. Neither the authors nor the publisher can be
responsible for changes in prices, exchange rates, business operations or other facts presented in good faith
herein.

Manufactured in the United States of America.

CONTENTS

Acknowledgments
Introduction

Chapter 1. How To Get Rolling: **17**
Acquiring a Van or Motorhome Abroad

Renting or Leasing
    Booking in Advance
    Independent Rental Agencies
    What It Will Cost
    Choosing the Right One
    Standard Equipment
Buying a Used Van or Motorhome
    What It Will Cost
    Dealers
    Where to Buy: Amsterdam, London,
        Frankfurt
Evaluating a Used Van or Motorhome
    A Word of Caution
    A Few Simple Tests
Buying a New Van or Motorhome
    How to Do It
    U.S. and Canadian Specifications
    Shipping Your New Vehicle Home
Bringing Your Own

Chapter 2. Prep Talk: Trip Planning Tips   **65**

When To Go
Booking Your Flight
Important Papers

Chapter 2. (continued)
Passport, Visas, International Driving
    Permit, International Camping Carnet
Changing Money
What To Take
    Checklists: Clothes, Motoring Needs,
        Health Needs, Fun and Comfort Items,
    Documents

**Chapter 3. Roads And Driving: Breezing
  Along Like a Native**   **75**

The Roads
    Motorway Etiquette: Country-By-Country
        Information
    Motorway Services
The Tourist Attraction from Hell
Crossing Borders
Asking Directions
The Driver-Navigator Relationship
City Driving
    Roundabouts
    Finding Fuel
Help On The Road: European Auto Clubs
Highway Signs
Maps and Guidebooks
Ferries
National Highway Laws and Emergency Phone
    Numbers

Chapter 4. Sleeping In The Best Places:　　103
　　Nightly Homesites

Finding a Campground
Procedure, Conveniences, Hours and Other
　　Customs
Dumpstations and Recycling
Laundry
Clothing Optional Campgrounds
Three Popular Campgrounds: London,
　　Paris, Munich
Country-by-Country Tips
Great Campgrounds: A Personal Sampler
Freecamping
How, Where, When To Do It
Great Freecamping Spots—A Personal Sampler

Chapter 5. "Where Do You...Uh....?"　　127

Finding Toilets: Self-Contained Vehicles,
　　Campgrounds, The Po, Other Resources
How To Ask In Six Languages
The Dreaded Squat
The Dragon
Bathing: Best Places, Techniques

Chapter 6. Language: Easier Than You Think　　135

English Spoken There
International Words: A List
Road Signs
Twenty-One Magic Words
Country-by-Country Tips
Crossed Wires: Words That Mean Something Else
Refreshment Savvy

Chapter 7. Money: Handling It Wisely   **145**

Quick Figuring
Money From Home: How To Get It
    Credit Cards
    Travelers Cheques
The Cost Of It All: Estimating Your Budget
Expensive, Inexpensive Countries

**Chapter 8. Bringing The Kids
(But Not The Dog)**   **149**

The Best Way To Travel With Children
Dog Laws, Considerations
Choosing The Right Rig For Your Family
Child Seat Belt Laws
What To Pack For Kids
Getting Ready
Campgrounds And Kids
Sights With High Kid Appeal

Chapter 9. Staying Safe And Healthy   **159**

On-The-Road Health Basics
    Exercise
    Jet Lag
    Doctors And Medicine
    Pedestrian Safety
    Fire Safety
Emotional Health
    The Van Choreography
    Dealing With Homesickness
Van And Motorhome Security
    Security Checklist

Chapter 10. Cooking On Wheels: Healthy, Cheap & Fun   **171**

Why Cook?
Your Rolling Kitchen
Tools To Bring
Settling Into Your Mini-Kitchen
Meal Plans, Including Picnics and Ferries
National Breakfasts
Efficient Cooking Techniques: Getting Your
    Moves Down

Chapter 11. Food Shopping Adventures: Another Facet of Europe   **179**

Outdoor Markets
Shopping Communication Technique
Weights And Change
Supermarkets
Closing Hours And Other Cautions
General Differences In European Foods
Shop Patterns
Country by Country Food Guide

Daily Trip Log: To Remember The Good Times 233

Index   **235**

ACKNOWLEDGMENTS

Over the years and kilometers, many people on both sides of the Atlantic have contributed to the creation of this book. We owe our thanks to all of them, but especially to:

Jacques Andrieu, Matthias and Heidi Blenck, Sjelden-Kristian Boeltl, David Braitman, Ed Buryn, Huseyin Duman, David Durrell, Maya and Viola Fink, Kristos and Stella Giandikiris, Rachael Hammond, Diane and David Henry, Bernard Hess, Thomas and Krista Jeier, Bill and Irene Jones, René Kluver, Ernst Marti, Arie and Renate Melchior, Gary and Lee Miller, Ioanna Mirisclavos, Theo Mirisclavos, Linda O'Farrell, Larry and Susan Rakow, Robert and Cathy Ryan, Lester and Barbara Sackett, Gunther and Marina Schmidt, Patrick Shea, Jerry and Ike Spurlock, Rick Steves, Colin and Charmayne Taylor, Andy Whitaker, Richard Woudenberg, and Joe Zucker.

"Go as a wayfarer open to all experience; go as a courier over the map of Europe, bearing messages to your secret self... The Age of Discovery is never over if *you* are the discoverer."

Ed Buryn
Vagabonding in Europe and North Africa

Introduction

The morning sky is ablaze with color as the sun rises over the Swiss Alps. The first rays to clear the peaks pierce the cool morning air and like a warm, gentle hand reach through a louvered window, waking a pair of sleepy adventurers. They stretch lazily, enjoying the deliciousness of the crisp breeze wafting in off the lake, the warm sun shining now into all the windows, and the snugness and privacy of their own home on the shores of Lake Geneva.

But they've enjoyed their free Swiss chalet long enough. They've been there a week; it's time to move on. The rolling French countryside calls. They consult the map and discover a back road that winds from the border all the way to Paris. So they fold up the inflatable boat and stow it under the seat, put away everything loose, and they're ready to head for the open road.

Their lakeside villa will become a private tour bus. It will stop wherever they want to stop. It will turn off onto interesting side roads. It will even allow them to change their minds and head for Provence and the Cote d'Azur.

After a day of marvelous sights and pleasant human encounters, they pull off the road and into a forest glade rosy with the glow of sunset. Dinner is a feast, cooked quickly and intimately in the van kitchen with foods more flavorful and fresher than those available at home. They dine by candlelight at their private table as Mozart serenades them from the tape deck.

Later, the well-fed couple spends the evening hours brushing up on their French and reading to each other from tour books about the fascinating experiences that wait for them along tomorrow's path. Tomorrow night, or the next night, when they are in Paris, they may opt for an evening on the town—their city clothes are hanging neatly in the closet—but tonight in the quiet forest they admire the stars and then snuggle gratefully into their own comfortable bed for a peaceful sleep as the sound of crickets wafts through the louvered window....

A pretty idyll. But is it just a fantasy? After all, everybody knows that European travel isn't this easy. You can't just go there and see what happens—you need itineraries, schedules, reservations. Right?

Wrong. With a van or motorhome, you have total flexibility. You can change your mind whenever a more interesting option appears. As examples, once we went to Europe with the general intention of driving down the boot of Italy, but it turned out to be a summer of record-breaking heat. So we went to Scandinavia instead, where everyone was delighted with the unaccustomed warmth. Another time we were driving in Germany one afternoon when we were struck with a powerful desire to have dinner in France. So we turned west, crossed the Rhine into Alsace, and had one of the most delicious meals of our lives in Strasbourg that evening.

Another thing everybody knows is that travel means hassling with luggage, check-out times at hotels, and train and bus schedules.

Not here it doesn't. You unpack only once, into your campervan's many handy cupboards and closets. Check-out time is whenever *you* feel like leaving—and it might not be until day after tomorrow. And you can spend your time seeing the beauties of Europe—not waiting on the platforms of endless train stations.

Everybody also is convinced that camping means roughing it. They probably have memories of sleeping on the cold ground on scouting trips. But your van is a clean, comfortable little house on wheels, not a drafty tent. European campgrounds are not wilderness outposts; they are pleasant grassy places with stores, cafes, and other civilized amenities. And every night you sleep in your own bed.

That same "everybody" suspects that driving in Europe is a nightmare of bad roads and wild drivers, and that trying to manage a motorhome under these conditions would be madness. Again, "everybody" is dead wrong. Most European highways and motorways are state of the art, and a campervan or small motorhome is as manageable as a car. European drivers must pass rigorous tests before they get their licenses and are usually quite skilled. Big-city traffic *can* be heavy and confusing, as at home, but you can avoid this problem easily by staying at a campground on the edge of town and riding the metro or a bus into the urban center.

And, finally, everybody *really* knows that a trip to Europe costs a fortune, right? Wrong once again. You can pay as much or as little for a van or motorhome as your pocket and your thirst for luxury dictate. We'll tell you where to find a wide range of rental vehicles from American-style motorhomes to that good old standby, the VW van. For trips of two months or more, you'll save by purchasing a vehicle from a dealer offering a buy-back guarantee. Again, we'll tell you who, where, and how. Actually, you can even make a profit if you time it right.

The first version of this book was called *Cheaper Than Staying Home,* because for us, in 1981, it was. We sublet our apartment and let somebody else pay the rent and the utilities, and went off on assignment to do a book about American street performers in Europe. We did our own cooking, which didn't count as an expense, because after all, you gotta eat at home, too. We freecamped behind the houses of jugglers or under the windows of guitarists, and that was okay, too, because it put us more in touch with our subjects—who soon became our friends. When we ran out of money for gas we found a good place and just stayed there awhile until our funds recovered. Eventually we sold our old van when we went home for almost as much as we'd paid for it three months earlier.

All this was just muddling through, because we had not been able to find a single book that told us how to van-travel in Europe. So we made mistakes—lots of them. We bought a terrible old wreck from a sinister mechanic in a back alley in London, and three weeks later it threw a rod and expired on a late Saturday afternoon as we were crossing the Rhine.

We didn't know how to register the vehicle or to buy insurance, so we didn't, a fact that now makes us pale. We crossed borders without changing money and then tried to use American dollars, a fact that now makes us blush. In short, we messed up at every turn, but we had a wonderful time anyway, and because we've done it wrong, we can tell you how to do it right.

We had so much fun that we went back the next year, and the next, and almost all the years since, for three or more months at a time. Gradually the kinks smoothed out as we got more practiced and knowledgeable. We wrote a little book to help other people with our hard won savvy, and our readers wrote and telephoned us by the hundreds to share their own experiences. Over the years we have upgraded our style and now travel in what would have struck us as luxury in the beginning—but we still choose a van, and we still have adventures.

Obviously, we are hooked on van and motorhome

travel, as are many Europeans. But is it for you? There are some trade-offs for all the good things. For the advantage of flexibility you must be willing to make your own decisions, to risk surprises good and bad—we'll tell you stories of both kinds. You must be willing to do your own driving—you'll find tips on European traffic know-how in chapter three. For the advantage of always having a place to sleep, you must pay some attention to the techniques of living in a small space—see chapter nine for a lesson on van choreography. For the opportunity to sample the Continental lifestyle and make European friends you must be willing to try a few words of foreign languages at least occasionally—for a magic list see chapter VI.

This book is a guide to the *techniques* of European van and motorhome travel. What this book is *not* is a destination guide. Other than mentioning a few of our favorite places we're not going to tell you where to go or what to see. Nor, obviously, are we going to give you lists of hotels and restaurants—you won't need them. Nor will we waste space on fillers like climate charts. What we *will* tell you is everything we think you need to know to rent, buy, sell, drive, and live in a camping vehicle in Europe and have a wonderful time doing it.

So there you have it. In exchange for very little money and a willingness to think for yourself, and with the help of this book, you can discover what Europeans have known for a generation: a motorhome or van is the key to *really* experiencing the delights and wonders of the Continent, not only economically, but with ease and comfort. Read on; we'll tell you how you too can do it.

A wide selection awaits at dealerships in Great Britain and Europe. (Photo by David Shore)

Chapter 1

How To Get Rolling:
Acquiring a Van or Motorhome Abroad

Finding a comfortable, reliable vehicle for your travels is not as complicated as you might think. If you prefer to rent a van or motorhome, your travel agent can book the exact model you want in advance of your trip, through a well-organized rental network. You can tap into this network yourself with the information in this chapter. We'll tell you what's available, how to order it, and about how much it will cost. We'll even make some recommendations, based on our own experience and feedback from readers of previous editions.

If you plan to spend two months or more in Europe, you'll be better off financially if you buy and resell a van or motorhome. You can pick up a good used one for roughly the same as you would pay for six weeks' rental—an adequate one for less than that—and you can get most or all of your money back when you sell it. You can even make a profit if you play it right. If you're in the market for a new European camper or car to take home, you can order it in advance, pick it up at the factory, and save enough on the purchase price to pay for the plane tickets.

Some people are very attached to their rigs at home and ask about shipping them to Europe and back. We don't recommend this unless you're planning a long stay and your rig is very special. But we'll tell you how to do it anyway.

And we'll tell you about registration and insurance in various countries, as well as how to ship a vehicle home (and the associated red tape).

RENTING OR LEASING

If you have less than two months to spend in Europe, renting will get you the most for your money. It's much quicker and easier than buying, and often less expensive than leasing. You'll get a new or nearly new rig, fully equipped with bedding, crockery, etc. Repairs, if any, are fully guaranteed. Registration and insurance are included in the package. You can book it in advance and have it ready and waiting when you step off the plane, so that you have only to hop in and go.

There are quite a few motorhome rental companies in the U.K. and on the Continent, and many different makes and models available. Choices range from the familiar VW Westfalia camper (called the "Joker" or "California" in Europe) through larger vans and "coach-built" motorhomes up to 25 feet long. These vehicles can be rented or, in some cases, leased.

Leasing can be arranged for you by agencies in North America (see list below). You get a brand new vehicle that is registered in your name. Insurance and registration are included, and no taxes apply in Belgium, France, and Spain. There is usually a 21-day minimum lease period. Check total cost; it may work out to be cheaper than renting.

BOOKING IN ADVANCE

The easiest way to rent a van or motorhome in Europe is to ask your travel agent to book one for you in advance. He or she will call a "wholesaler," a broker of many different travel-related things. These wholesalers make bookings of all types, and most deal only with travel agents, not with individual customers. Their reasoning on this is that customers take up their time with questions, while travel agents make most of the actual bookings.

Many travel agents can answer questions about vans and motorhomes for rent or lease, but if you want more specific information, there are agencies who will talk to you. They include:

- Avis
  (800) 331-1084 (US)
  (800) 879-2847 (Canada)

- Campanje
  (209) 245-3129 (Worldwide)

- DER Tours
  (800) 937-1236 (US)
  (416) 695-1209 (Worldwide)

- Eliza Travel
  (613 03) 787 7194 (Worldwide)
  (008) 338817 (Australia)

- Foremost Euro-Car
  (213) 872-2226 (Worldwide)
  (800) 272-3299 (US)
  (800) 253-3876 (Canada)

- Global Motorhome Travel
  (310) 318-9995 (Worldwide)
  (800) GMT-EURO (US & Canada)

- Hertz
  (800) 654-3001 (US & Canada)

- Owasco
  (800) 263-2676 (Ontario)
  (416) 668-9383 (Worldwide)

- Tradesco Tours
  (310) 649-5808 (Worldwide)

These agencies will book a motorhome rental for you through selected dealerships in the U.K. and Europe. The dealers have adjusted their prices to match the uniform rates advertised and guaranteed by the booking agents. Actual motorhome models and configurations may vary, but quality, size, and equipment supplied have been standardized. Most agencies are booked up in summer, so call early.

INDEPENDENT RENTAL AGENCIES

You can make direct contact with rental dealers in Europe or the U.K., whether or not they are part of the booking networks listed above. It takes a bit more effort, but most of them will send you brochures and other specific information so that you can do some comparison shopping. You might even find lower rates. Some of the best dealers we've found are listed here:

(When phoning from within the same country, add "0" prefix)

Netherlands

* A-Point Rent a Camper
  PB 12888
  1100 AW Amsterdam
  Tel: (20) 6964964
  Fax: (20) 6975270

* Achilles Campers
  Walenburghof 17
  3033 HK Rotterdam
  Tel: (10) 465 6400

- Braitman & Woudenberg
  Droogbak 3-4
  1013 GE Amsterdam
  Tel: (20) 622 11 68
  Fax: (20) 620 38 55

- Campanje
  Corn. Dirkzstraat 171
  3506 GH Utrecht
  Tel: (30) 447070
  Fax: (30) 420981

Great Britain

- Cabervans Luxury Motorhome Hire
  Caberfeidh, Cloch Road
  Gourock PA19 1BA
  Scotland
  Tel/Fax: (475) 38775

- Motorhome Rentals (Europe) Ltd.
  Lowood Garage
  12 Kings Avenue
  Clapham, London SW4
  Tel: (71) 720 6492
  Fax: (71) 720 6721

- Pullman Motor Caravan Hire
  22 Wolvey Road
  Bulkington, Coventry CV12 9JU
  Tel: (203) 314491

- Sunseeker Rentals Ltd
  27d Stable Way
  London W10 6QX
  Tel: (81) 960 5747
  Fax: (81) 960 1414

- Turners of London
  11a Barry Road
  East Dulwich, London SE22 OHZ
  Tel: (81) 693 1132
  Fax: (81) 693 1134

France

- Avis Car Away
  60, Rue de Caen
  92400 Courbevoic (Paris)
  Tel: (1) 43.34.15.81
  Fax: (1) 47.68.77.94

Germany

- Moser im Kunze Haus
  Berner Str. 99
  D-W6000 Frankfurt am Main 50
  Tel: (69) 5072005, 5083250
  Fax: (69) 5072021

- Ralf Moses
  Kurt-Schumacher-Str. 1
  D-W6392 Neu Anspach (Frankfurt)
  Tel: (800) GMT-EURO

- Trueblood RV GmbH
  Am Kunzengarten 15
  65936 Frankfurt/Main
  Tel: (60) 3371411
  Fax: (60) 3372119

- WVD Wohnmobile
  Gewerbestr. 9
  7800 Freiburg-Opfingen
  Tel: (7664) 5552
  Fax: (7664) 59386

Greece

- Camper Caravans S.A.
  4 Nikis St.
  Athens 105 63
  Tel: (3230) 552-5

- Motor Caravans Club
  330 Athinon Str.
  Haidari
  Athens
  Tel: (1) 58 12 103

Italy

- CamperSi
  Via Pontina 407
  00128 Rome
  Tel. (6) 5074054

- Freedom Holiday
  Via C. Colombo 2339
  00144 Rome
  Tel: (6) 50914212

- Centro Milano Caravan
  Via le Lombardia 96
  20052 Monza (Milan)
  Tel: (39) 737373

Switzerland

- Reisebüro Marti
  3283 Kallnach (Bern)
  Tel: (32) 822822
  Fax: (32) 822123, 820381

- Moby Campers
  Moslistrasse 12
  4532 Feldbrunnen (Solothurn)
  Tel: (65) 22 9610

- Petersen's Motorhomes
  10 Route De Lausanne
  1180 Rolle (Geneva)
  Tel: (21) 8254659

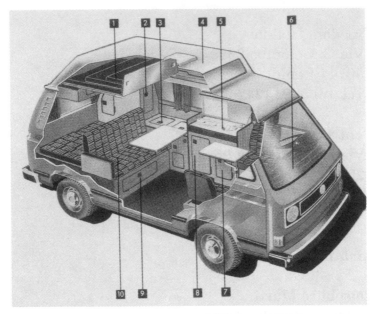

The VW Westfalia Joker III. (Courtesy Braitman & Woudenberg)

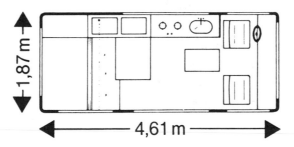

1,87 m

4,61 m

1 Upper double berth
2 Wardrobe
3 Storage
4 Solid high-built roof
5 Kitchen unit with running water and 2 burner gas stove
6 Stereo cassette radio
7 42 litre refrigerator
8 Food storage
9 Storage for bedding
10 Sofa-seat converts into double-bed

Braitman & Woudenberg

Droogbak 4ᴬ	**1013 GE Amsterdam**	**Telephone 020 - 622 11 68**
P.O. Box 1891	**1000 BW Amsterdam**	**Telefax** ● **020 - 620 38 55**

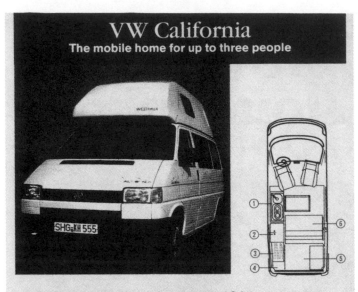

VW California
The mobile home for up to three people

① Kitchen unit with running water and 2-burner gas stove
② 40-litre cool box (12 V) · ③ Wardrobe · ④ Storage
⑤ Upper double berth · ⑥ Sofa seat converts into double berth

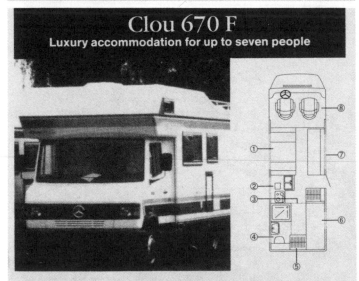

Clou 670 F
Luxury accommodation for up to seven people

① Seating unit converts into double berth · ② Kitchen unit with sink
3-burner gas stove and 103-litre refrigerator ③ Sliding door
④ Bath unit with flushing toilet, wash basin and shower
⑤ Wardrobe ⑥ Seating unit converts into upper and lower berths
⑦ Storage compartment · ⑧ Double berth in the alcove

WHAT IT WILL COST

Although there are many different rental agencies in the U.K. and Europe, their rates are roughly comparable, as are the vehicles themselves. You can rent a fully equipped VW California at low season (October-April) for about $450 to $550 per week. Add another $60 per week in May or September, and another $60 in "high season" (June, July, and August). Automatic transmission is available for an additional $40 per week. Taxes are often included.

A larger motorhome that sleeps four, five, or six adults can be rented for as little as $567 per week in low season, $700 per week in May or September, and $840 in high season.

These rates are approximate, as they vary from agency to agency and are often quoted in foreign currencies, against which the value of the dollar fluctuates daily. Taxes average 15 to 20 per cent, depending on the country where you rent the vehicle. Insurance is usually included, but there is normally a collision deductible. This can be waived by purchasing Collision Damage Waiver (CDW) at $10-15 per day. It is often included if you use a Gold credit card.

CHOOSING THE RIGHT ONE

The mainstay of the industry, and the least expensive choice on most companies' price lists, is the VW California. It comes with diesel or gasoline engine, with either a canvas-walled pop-top or a rigid fiberglass high top. (The latter is quieter and cozier in bad weather and has more storage space but is too tall to enter most parking garages or pass under the occasional low bridge.) The VW drives and parks like a car, gets over 20 MPG, and is surprisingly roomy and comfortable. For two adults and two children, it's ideal.

EUROPE BY VAN AND MOTORHOME

Sales and Rental
The best prices and rates on VW-campers

Some of our special features:
* custom-built VW-Campervans
* buy-back guarantee up to 75%
* all-inclusive rental rates

* free pick-up from the Airport
* personal service:
    We really help you get on your way!

Corn. Dirkszstraat 171
P.O. Box 9332
3506 GH Utrecht
The Netherlands
Tel. 31-30-447070
Fax 31-30-420981

U.S. representative:
3081 Little Spur Road
Somerset, CA 95684

Tel./Fax (209) 245-3129

Larger van campers, like the Ford Transit or the similar Fiat and Peugeot vans, are popular among private owners but are less often found on the rental market these days. They offer a bit more room than the VW, and come with petrol or diesel engines.

The next step up is called the four-berth, and it's comparable to an American Mini: a motorhome body on a van chassis. It normally has a shower and toilet, two double beds, and more living and storage space than a van.

The six- and seven-berth models are quite roomy, but they're a bit large and ungainly for the narrow streets of European cities and the tiny country lanes of England. You'll pay higher campground fees and ferry fares, and you'll need a special driver's license if your rig weighs more than 3.5 tons. And the rental rates can be high. These rigs are best suited for two families to share.

In general, it's best to choose the smallest vehicle that you and your travel mate(s) will be comfortable with. Much of your time will be spent driving, and the more maneuverability you have on those narrow, sometimes confusing streets, the more comfortable you'll be under way.

STANDARD EQUIPMENT

You can expect your rental van or motorhome to come with at least the following equipment:

Beds for two or more
Refrigerator
Gas stove
Kitchen sink with water supply and pump
Kitchen counter space
Dining table
Cooking utensils
Crockery and cutlery
Food storage space
Linens and bedding
Heater in living space
Radio (many with cassette player)
Standard automotive heater
Spare tire, jack, emergency warning triangle

Some rental companies charge one-time fees for such things as linens, toilet chemicals, and cleaning. Others do not. Some may give you too much gear. Weed out what you don't need and leave it with them; space in a van is valuable and limited.

BUYING A USED VAN OR MOTORHOME

If you're planning to stay in Europe for more than two

months, you can save money by buying, instead of renting, a van or motorhome. With a buy-back guarantee, the longer you stay, the more you save. And if you sell it on the open market, you can even make a profit if the season is right.

It's not as difficult or risky as you might think. We'll show you how to evaluate a used vehicle and how to further protect yourself.

You can buy from a dealer or from a private owner. There are advantages and disadvantages to both. Some dealers offer buy-back agreements and mechanical warranties; private owners offer lower prices. You get what you pay for. We'll tell you how and where to buy and sell wisely.

WHAT IT WILL COST

A clean, well-equipped, mechanically sound VW camper can be purchased from a dealer for about $5,000 and up. Dealers sell late-model Jokers (VW Westfalias) for about $10,000 and up. Prices increase with size, newness, and equipment. Buy-back agreements usually promise a 50 to 70 per cent return, if the vehicle is brought back within a year in the same general condition as when it left the dealership.

DEALERS

The quickest and easiest way to find a suitable home on wheels is to go to one of the agencies that sell them. Their buy-backs and warranties are the principal advantages of dealing with them instead of private sellers. It's a very competitive market, and many dealers have gone out of business in the past few years. Only the best have survived. They are listed below.

Various dealers offer different services and products. For example, Braitman & Woudenberg in Amsterdam sell VW and Ford campers from their rental fleet, as well as others they buy and recondition. They make sure each vehicle is mechanically sound as well as cosmetically appealing and comfortable. They employ carpenters and upholsterers to refurbish interiors, and will modify them to your specifications.

For the extra money you spend with a dealer, you get:

1. Guaranteed Buy-back

A very reassuring arrangement. You know at the start that you can sell the vehicle on the day you are to leave Europe, instead of wasting a desperate week at the end of your trip trying to unload it. This is especially important if you will be leaving at or near the end of the travel season, when everybody is selling and nobody

is buying. Here is where the higher purchase price pays off. You know exactly how much you will get back: the percentage you and the dealer agreed upon. But you are free to sell the vehicle to someone else if you so choose.

2. Mechanical Warranty

This is something you can never hope for when buying from a private owner, who hopes to never see you or his van again. On the contrary, the dealership plans to buy this vehicle back, so they have an interest in its mechanical fitness. And since they are making sure it is fit, they can guarantee it. The interior equipment should be included in the warranty.

3. Professional Facilities

A warranty is worthless if the seller can't back it up. A good dealership has a service shop equipped to service and repair your vehicle. It should also be able to authorize repairs, if necessary, at professional facilities throughout Europe and Great Britain, or be willing to reimburse you for repairs you must pay for yourself.

4. Reputation

Any business establishment is interested in maintaining a good name with satisfied customers. Unscrupulous dealers do exist, unfortunately, but eventually word gets around. We invite your comments and recommendations about specific dealers for use in future editions.

5. Registration and Insurance

A dealer should help you in properly registering your vehicle. Some dealers sell insurance, and you can have everything taken care of with a minimum of time and effort expended.

WHERE TO BUY

Amsterdam and London are the two most popular—and most logical—places to start a European adventure, and both cities have highly developed van and motorhome markets. Many English-speaking travelers fly into London first because the airfare is often a bit cheaper and they anticipate no language problems. But in Amsterdam nearly everyone under fifty speaks English, and the generally lower prices there make up for the slightly higher airfare. Most used vans in the Netherlands are in better mechanical condition than in Britain.

Frankfurt is another popular destination where you can buy or rent a very good van or motorhome. Dealer prices are a bit higher there, but so is quality, and English is spoken there, too. We'll cover these three cities in detail.

AMSTERDAM

Amsterdam boasts a large and diverse selection of vans and motorhomes. The quality of the rolling stock is generally higher here than in London, and registration is handled more quickly and easily. It's a compact city with good public transportation, and getting around is easy.

Dealer Listing

The following is a list of dealers who sell campers and motorhomes in Amsterdam and vicinity. You may wish to contact them in advance of your trip to see what's available and who can best suit your needs. To phone from within the Netherlands, dial "0" before the number.

- A-Point Rent-A-Camper
  Kollenbergweg 11
  Amsterdam Z O
  Tel: (20) 696 49 64, fax (20) 697 52 70
  (VWs)
- Braitman & Woudenberg
  Droogbak 3-4
  1013 GE Amsterdam
  Tel: (20) 622 11 68, fax (20) 620 38 55
  (VWs, Fords and motorhomes)
- Campanje
  Corn. Dirkszstraat 171
  P.O. Box 9332
  3506 GH Utrecht
  Tel: (30) 44 70 70, fax (30) 42 09 81
  (VWs)

Private Sellers

Private owners advertise vans and motorhomes in newspaper classified ads, or just park them on the street with "Te Koop" (for sale) signs in the windows. A good place to look for the latter group is on the streets radiating out from the Central Station, or on the other side of town near the Olympic Stadium. Organized van markets occur from time to time in Amsterdam, Utrecht, and other Dutch cities. Check with the VVV for current locations and dates.

The most newspaper ads are to be found in *De Telegraaf*, a large daily in Amsterdam. They are in Dutch, however, and unless you have a friend who can translate the ads, you'll have to call each one. The

*The Ford Transit, basis for many a camper conversion.
(Photo by David Shore)*

owner will probably speak English and will be able to answer all of your questions.

Making sure you get a good one is not difficult if you follow the procedures recommended under "Evaluating a Used Van or Motorhome" later in this chapter. Private sellers are usually easy to deal with, especially if they're travelers like you and their plane leaves for home tomorrow.

APK Sticker

The Netherlands has a motor vehicle safety inspection which is required for registration and insurance. The vehicle you buy should have a valid APK sticker. Check the expiration date. Ask for the papers that go with the sticker to avoid fakes. A new sticker will cost 50 guilders, plus the cost of any repairs required. Driving without one can get you a fine of 120 guilders and confiscation of the vehicle. *Note:* a valid APK sticker does not necessarily mean that the engine, transmission and drive train parts are good.

Registration and Insurance

To register your newly-purchased vehicle, take the title and registration papers to the nearest post office. The clerk will transfer these documents to your name while you wait. Insurance can be arranged through a camper dealer who sells it, or through an insurance agency listed in the yellow pages (Gouden Gids) under "Verzekering."

LONDON

There are quite a few dealers and private sellers in London. One problem you'll find here is that most of the vehicles for sale have right-hand drive (RHD). This may be better for driving in Great Britain (once you get used to it), but it makes driving more difficult on the

Large American motorhomes can be rented or purchased in Great Britain and Europe. (Photo by David Shore)

Continent. RHD is found mostly on larger motorhomes; you'll have better luck finding a left-hand-drive vehicle among the VWs and Fords. Still, most of them will be RHD.

Dealer Listing

The following is a list of dealers in London. You may wish to contact them in advance of your trip to see what's available and who can best suit your needs. To phone from within Great Britain, dial "0" before the number.

* Bilbo's Trading Company
  Marlfield, Eastbourne Rd (A22)
  South Godstone, Surrey RH9 8JQ
  Tel: (342) 892499/893149
  (All VW campers, RHD & LHD, no buy-back)

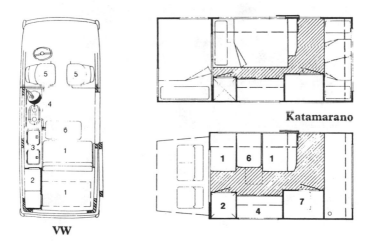

Katamarano

VW

1 Bed/Seat
2 Storage
3 Fridge
4 Kitchen, 2 burner stove etc.
5 Swivel Seats
6 Table
7 Shower + toilet

(Courtesy Braitman & Woudenberg)

The Aussie-Kiwi Van Mart (Photo by David Shore)

- Bromley Motor Caravans
  55-65 Abbey Road
  Belvedere DA17 5DG
  Tel: (81) 311 3500
  (Larger rigs, all RHD, buy-back negotiable)

- Turners of London
  11a Barry Road
  East Dulwich, London SE22 0HX
  Tel: (81) 693 1132
  Fax: (81) 693 1134
  (Various models, RHD & LHD, buy-back negotiable)

Private Sellers

Aussie-Kiwi Van Mart

At London's Aussie-Kiwi Van Mart, you can find a comprehensive selection of vans and motorhomes, most of them owned by travelers from Australia and New Zealand. They are all grouped together in one place for direct comparison and competition. It's considered the cheapest way for young people to take the grand tour, and it is world-famous, though it has been moved several times (and may be moved again). Vans and motorhomes bearing English license plates and AUS or NZ stickers on their tails are seen all over Europe, North Africa, and the Near East.

The market is an unofficial cluster of rigs parked along Market Road, near the Caledonia Road Station on the Underground. Many vehicles there are right-hand drive, and some show signs of a long, hard life. But if you find one that appeals to you, check it out with our Evaluation Checklist. If the price is right, you could pick up a bargain.

Classified Ads

Another way to buy from a private owner is through the classified ads in newspapers and magazines. The best ones in London are found in the *Exchange and Mart* and the *Auto Trader,* popular weekly publications that sell for about one pound. Other good sources are *TNT, LAW,* and *LAM,* free magazines aimed at Aussies and Kiwis, available at newsstands near Underground stations in central London.

M.O.T. Certificate

The Ministry of Transport (M.O.T.) annually inspects motor vehicles for safety and roadworthiness, and issues an M.O.T. certificate if it passes. When you buy a vehicle, make sure it has one that will be valid as long as you want to use the vehicle in the U.K. If it needs a

(Courtesy Eliza Travel Pty. Ltd.)

new M.O.T., you must pay for the inspection and any repairs required. It's an important bargaining point.

Registration and Insurance

Dealers and private sellers should help you to properly register your vehicle, and to arrange insurance. The Automobile Club of Great Britain (AA) sells insurance, and can also help you to register a vehicle you buy from a private seller.

In any case, you must have a *Bill of Sale*. This is usually hand-written by the seller, since there is no official form. It should describe the vehicle and show the vehicle identification number and the license number, and should be signed by the seller and dated. It should also include the price you paid, as it will also serve as a receipt.

You should also get a *Vehicle Registration Document* from the seller, and take both documents to the Department of Transport, Vehicle Registration Office, 1 Zoar Street, London SE1 OSY. This is in central London, near the London Bridge station of the Underground. While you wait, they will issue a *Certificate of Registration*, which is proof of ownership.

FRANKFURT

For a more centrally located starting point, many travelers head for Frankfurt. It's a popular destination, being an airline hub for Lufthansa and Condor, which offer many low-cost flights from North America. Frankfurt's central location makes it convenient to Berlin and eastern Europe, as well as Austria and southern Europe.

It's also a good place to buy a van or motorhome. You can find good vehicles at motorhome agencies and general used-car dealers there. You can look for a used vehicle

*The Knaus Traveller 625 sleeps 4 adults. Turbo Diesel
engine, Power Steering, 5-speed manual shift.*

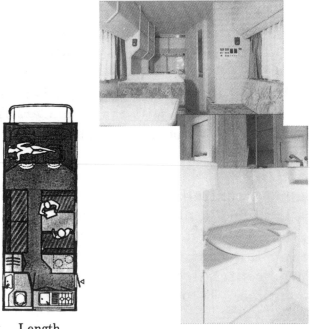

Length
20 Feet

(Courtesy Global Motorhome Travel, Inc.)

at the many U.S. and Canadian military bases nearby, on university campuses, or at weekend sales on drive-in movie lots. And of course, there are classified ads.

Dealer Listing

The following is a list of dealers in Frankfurt. You may wish to contact them in advance of your trip to see what's available and who can best suit your needs. To phone from within Germany, dial "0" before the number.

* Moser im Kunze-Haus
  Berner Str. 99
  D-W6000 Frankfurt am Main 50
  Tel: (69) 5072005
  Fax: (69) 5072021
  (4-6-berth & larger motorhomes)

* Ralf Moses
  Kurt-Schumacher-Str. 1
  D-W6392 Neu Anspach
  Tel: (800) GMT-EURO
  (4-6-berth & larger motorhomes)

* Trueblood RV GmbH
  Am Kunzengarten 15
  D-65936 Frankfurt/M
  Tel: (69) 345354
  Fax: (69) 343872
  (VWs, 4-6-berth & larger motorhomes)

Private Sellers
Weekend Markets

A large selection of motor vehicles of all types can be found at weekend sales (usually Sunday), often located on outdoor drive-in movie lots in Frankfurt and other major cities. Ask for the *Autokino Markt*.

There hundreds of privately-owned used cars, trucks, vans, and motorhomes are lined up for your inspection. The owners are usually on hand, and many speak English. Prices are flexible and competition is keen. Sellers are happy to allow you to climb in and out and around and try everything out. You can even take it for a test drive. This will give you a good feel for the type of conveyance you want to spend your vacation in. There is no tax when you buy there, and registration, license, and insurance can be handled in one day at the post office.

Universities

Elsewhere in Germany the universities are good places to look. You will often find several vans in various states of conversion parked near the *Mensa* (student union) with *"Verkaufen"* (for sale) signs in their windows. Inside the Mensa are bulletin boards full of ads. The prices are usually low, and most German students speak fluent English.

Classified Ads

Newspaper ads are another source, though they may be difficult to read if you don't understand German. A bilingual friend can be helpful in reading the ads and talking to sellers who don't speak English. *Frankfurter Allgemeine* is the newspaper with the most ads.

TUV Sticker

Germans take their machinery seriously, and unsound vehicles are not tolerated. All vehicles must pass a rigid inspection for safety and roadworthiness every two years. It's called *Technischer UberwachungsVerein* (TUV). It's similar to the APK in Holland and the M.O.T. in England, but it was the original.

Check the rear license plate for the round, colored sticker in the center. It shows the date when the next TUV inspection is due, which of course tells you how recently the vehicle passed the last one.

EVALUATING A USED VAN OR MOTORHOME

A WORD OF CAUTION

A private owner may honestly believe that he or she is selling you a good vehicle at a fair price. But unless that person is a qualified mechanic, you can't be sure there will be no unpleasant surprises down the road. The money you save could turn out to be a false economy. Use this list and be careful.

A FEW SIMPLE TESTS

When you've found a vehicle you like, whether it's in the hands of a private owner or a dealer, there a few simple tests you can make. They will give you a fairly good idea of the condition of its vital parts. Run it through this checklist. If it passes all of these tests, It's probably a good buy:

1. Body Language

The condition of the body can tell you a lot about the kind of care and maintenance the rest of the vehicle has received. If dents, rust spots, broken lights, etc., have gone unrepaired, ask why. If it has new paint, ask why. A vehicle less than ten years old shouldn't require it, except for custom bodywork or damage repairs. Look closely at the texture of the body surfaces. If it looks like it was molded out of putty, that may be the case. Look for file marks and lumps. Knock lightly with your fist all around the body and listen for changing sounds. A little bit of solid plastic filler sound is not bad; scratches and dents are a part of life. But if you find a lot of it, especially around door frames or other structural areas, this vehicle has been seriously hurt.

2. Rust

Check for excessive rust. The rocker panels (below the doors) are usually the first parts to rust through. On a VW, the jacking points are located here, and if they're rusted out, you won't be able to jack up the van except by using a non-VW jack on the bumper. On other makes, the rocker panels are not as important as the frame and floor pan, but they can tip you off to more critical problems underneath.

3. Interior

Of course you'll want to check all the mechanical things thoroughly anyway, but starting with the interior lets you find out if you like being in the rig in the first place. That's the most important part, after all. You're going to be living in this thing for the whole time you're in Europe. Making you comfortable and happy is its primary responsibility. That's what separates it from all the impersonal, uncomfortable hotel rooms it will replace.

With that in mind, you can start checking out the livability of your prospective home on wheels. Pull down, set up, unfold, or do whatever is necessary to get the bed into sleeping trim. If it's a motorhome with permanent beds, that's good. If it's a van camper, the bed should be easy to work.

Look for a built-in two-burner stove with a detachable propane tank. These stoves are odorless and convenient, and light instantly. Propane refills are available all over Europe at campgrounds, service stations, and many stores.

An electric refrigerator is better than an icebox, of course. If the vehicle has one, that's a definite plus. Modern ones can be switched (or switch automatically) from 12-volt battery power (while driving) to 240 volts (on campground hookups) to propane (for freecamping). Check for this feature.

A sink with water supply, pump, and drain is a necessity, even if you don't plan to cook. It makes the difference between roughing it (with bottles of water) and being at home anywhere. Make sure the drain works well and the water tank is easy to fill.

Check out the storage space. How efficiently is it used? Can you fit in all your gear and keep it organized in a convenient way? Vans and motorhomes vary a lot on this point, as do personal needs. Use your own judgment.

An AM-FM, or multi-band (short wave) radio is nice to have, not only while driving, but in the evenings. The BBC features comprehensive news, talk, and entertainment programming that will brighten up evenings in the campground. You'll want a cassette player, too, if you bring your favorite tapes from home.

4. Mechanicals

Once you're satisfied with the interior and general appearance of your candidate, it's time to see if it will be a trouble-free transportation device. After all, a major advantage of this mode of travel is being able to go and stop wherever *you* want, not where *it* decides.

Starting

The engine should start easily when you turn the key. If you have to crank it a long time, the reason may be that it's been sitting for a while and there's no fuel in the carburetor. The seller should have started it before you came to see it. Ruling out that condition, hard starting could indicate a weak battery, spark plugs needing replacement, valves needing adjustment or a valve job, or an engine needing a complete overhaul. You'll be able to feel that one when (if) it does start and you get rolling.

Brakes

Before you get rolling too fast, check the brakes. Just step on the pedal and see if the vehicle stops. The pedal should be at least three inches off the floor. Step on it a few more times and see if it pumps up to a higher level. If so, keep your foot on it. If it slowly sinks down again, there is a leak or air in the system, and the brakes are not to be trusted.

Driving Feel

Does it feel good to drive? If this is your first experience driving a van or motorhome, it will feel strange, of course, but look for smoothness, solidity, and ease of control. Don't expect neck-snapping acceleration, but you'll feel it if it's strong and healthy. It will sound smooth, too. It should idle calmly and quietly, and not threaten to die every time you stop at a traffic light. It should start up without stumbling.

Clutch

It should start up without shuddering, too. If the clutch doesn't engage smoothly, the pressure plate could be warped, the transmission mounts loose, or the fly-wheel about to fly off. The clutch pedal should not have more than two inches of play. Push it in with your hand to make sure. To really test the clutch, set the parking brake with the engine running, put it in first gear, and slowly let out the clutch as if to drive away. It should stall the engine and not slip. Do this just once; it's not good for the clutch. This test also tells you about the effectiveness of the parking brake.

Transmission

Run it up through the gears. Does it shift smoothly, easily, and solidly? Of course, you have to get used to the shift pattern. But if it's hard to get into gear after you've gotten used to it, there's a problem. It might mean worn synchronizers or worse. Test it for popping out of gear by going through all the gears including reverse. Back it up and take your foot off the gas and see it pops out. Try all the gears that way, accelerating up to about the speed at which you would normally shift up, but don't. Just take your foot off the gas. In fourth gear, take it up to about 90 km/h. If it pops out of any gear when you lift your foot, the transmission is no good.

Heater

When the engine is warmed up, check the heater and defroster. You'll need them. If it's a VW, and you smell exhaust fumes, the heat exchangers need replacement. This can be expensive or dangerous. Repairs could be minor if the vehicle has a water-cooled engine. If it's not a VW and you smell fumes, there's an exhaust leak somewhere. This can be expensive and dangerous, too. Check the exhaust system. There may be just a small leak that can be patched.

Lights, Wipers, Equipment

Check the lights, including turn signals and brake lights, and make sure they're working properly. Windshield wipers, too, are very important in Europe, so check them, too. Also make sure there's a spare tire, jack, emergency triangle, and necessary tools.

Engine Compression

You've already felt for the power and smoothness of the engine and listened for unseemly noises. Blue oil smoke from the exhaust is an indication of excessive wear and makes itself readily apparent. Now for the real engine test.

You should have a compression tester with you. If not, you can get one in Europe. It will tell you if the engine is in good condition and will last out your trip without problems, or if it's about to expire. Blue oil smoke could indicate worn piston rings, but dirty oil can cause the same symptom. The compression test will tell you for sure.

With the engine off, pull out all the spark plugs, making sure you keep them in order so that you can put them back in the same cylinders. Look at the electrodes. Are they all the same color? They should be close. They should be beige or slightly darker, or even slightly grayish. If one or more is black and gooey, it is oil-fouled, indicating bad rings (but black and fluffy simply means and overrich fuel mixture). The compression test will show that, too.

Hold the compression tester firmly in each spark plug hole (or screw it in, if you have that type), and hold it there while someone turns the ignition key, cranking the engine over six times or more. Check all the cylinders this way, writing down or remembering readings.

They should be within five pounds of each other.

If they are all over 100 pounds, the engine is in good shape. With proper care it should give you a trouble-free tour of Europe. Readings slightly below 100, if uniform, are not too bad, but anything less indicates that this is an engine you don't want to depend on too heavily.

A van or motorhome that has gotten this far in the testing is doing well. We've considered all the important things — the ones that could stop you. This test is thorough enough for a permanent purchase, but for service like we are demanding from our machinery, it's good to know that everything is going to hold up. That's much more likely, of course, if you take it easy. Drive gently and it will treat you right.

BUYING A NEW VAN OR MOTORHOME

If you're in the market for a new European van or motorhome, or even a car, you have an excellent opportunity to combine the purchase with your vacation. You'll enjoy both more, and you'll save money on both. To begin with, you'll save about ten per cent on the purchase price. That's an average figure, of course. In the case of a new VW Westfalia camper, for instance, the saving is enough to buy two round-trip air tickets from North America to Germany.

A major advantage is that you get exactly what you want. Your vehicle is built to your specifications and includes only the options you order. There's no need to pay for your dealer's "flooring" charge, which is simply his overhead.

If you order a VW camper, you can begin enjoying it as soon as you pick it up at the factory. Along with a free stay in the Westfalia campground, there is a complete factory tour and other amenities. Many other manufacturers have well-organized programs like this for buyers taking delivery at the factory. So well-organized, in fact, that it's almost as easy as buying from your local dealer.

It's not even unusual any more; in recent years thousands of European vans and cars have left the factory in North American hands. There is usually a factory tour, refreshments and presentation of the vehicle included. Of course, if you don't care to go through all that fanfare, you can arrange to pick up your new car or van at another location. This will involve an extra fee in most cases.

HOW TO DO IT

There are two ways, basically, of buying a new car or van for delivery in Europe. You can order it through your local dealer or through one of several independent agencies who specialize in just this sort of thing. They can order almost any make and model available for export. Contact them and they will mail you catalogs and complete instructions. Here are the major ones:

- Foremost Euro-Car
  5658 Sepulveda Blvd., Suite 201
  Van Nuys, CA 91411
  Tel: (213) 872-2226
  (800) 272-3299 (US)
  (800) 253-3876 (Canada)
  Fax: (818) 786-1249

- Shipside Tax Free Cars
  600 B Lake St.
  Ramsey, NJ 07446
  Tel. (201) 818-0400

Ordering

If you choose to order through a dealer, you can look at his catalogs and option lists, haggle a while and make your best deal, set a delivery date, sign a lot of papers, and put down a deposit.

If you are ordering through an independent, you can either go to their office and do the same things you would at the dealer's, or you can do it all by mail. The independent must order through a dealer anyway, and the price is the same to both. The difference to you depends on the deal you make, your dealer's ability to do it right, and the relative convenience of each.

Payment

When you place your order, you will be asked for a deposit of approximately three to five per cent of the total price. The balance is required 35 days before delivery. Financing may or may not be handled by the dealer or independent broker, or you may arrange your own.

Insurance

Vehicle insurance in Europe is referred to as "Green Card" insurance. It is required throughout Europe and the U.K. The VW factory will sell you liability and collision coverage on the vehicle you purchase.

You can also buy insurance at any insurance company in the country where the vehicle is registered. Or you may be able to prearrange coverage through your agent at home.

Warranty

Your new vehicle will come with the same warranty offered wherever it is sold. It's an international warranty with provisions in force throughout the world. Any dealer of that marque must honor it.

SPECIFICATIONS

The vehicle you receive will be an export model, complete with all the safety and emissions-control modifications required where you live. A catalytic converter, required on all U.S. and Canadian vehicles, is included, but may not be installed. It cannot be used in all countries of Europe, because it requires unleaded fuel, which is not available in some places where you might wish to drive. So it must and will be installed by the manufacturer before your vehicle is shipped home.

SHIPPING YOUR NEW VEHICLE HOME

After enjoying your new van or car in Europe during your vacation, you will have to drop it off at a predetermined port location (some manufacturers, like VW, will allow you to drop it off at one of a certain number of specified dealers in various cities of the home country) for shipment home. The shipment itself is arranged in advance by your dealer or the factory. Some manufacturers include shipment in the price of the vehicle, while others do not. In such cases you must pay the shipping charge. This can range from about $1000 to $2000 for east coast ports, $500 extra for west coast delivery. Mandatory marine insurance can cost from $300 to $800. Marine insurance does not cover personal possessions inside the vehicle, which are likely to be stolen. Shipping takes about three weeks to the east coast, five weeks to the west.

TAXES

Germany collects a refundable export tax (about $500 on a VW camper) which will be returned to you when the vehicle is actually put on the boat. You have up to one year to deliver it for shipment, during which time you may drive it in and out of Germany at will, although it must cross the border within the first six months. The vehicle will come with oval license plates, which you can keep as souvenirs if you fill out some forms. Germany is the only European country with an export tax on its motor vehicles.

You can avoid paying sales tax in many states and provinces if you keep your new van or car on European soil for at least 91 days. After that you can bring it home and register it sales-tax-free as a used vehicle (at a lower rate of duty).

BRINGING YOUR OWN

Unless you plan to stay in Europe for a long time and you're very attached to your rig, it's not very practical to think about shipping it over there. You have to ship it back home, too, and it's sort of like throwing $3,000 to $8,000 into the ocean. You must put up with long delays, lots of paperwork, port officials, customs officials, inconvenience, possible damage, possible pilferage, and extra fees for everything. It may take you only hours to fly to the European city of your choice, but it will take your vehicle a month or more, and it will arrive at a place where you probably wouldn't go otherwise.

For example, transporting a small van from Los Angeles to Bremen or Antwerp (the cheapest European ports) will cost about $3,000 round-trip for a container shared with two other vehicles. Insurance, port fees, customs fees, brokerage fees, documentation fees, storage fees, etc., are extra. A larger motorhome will require a flatbed or open-top container costing $3,500 to $4,000 one-way.

Unleaded fuel is not available in many parts of

Europe, and unless you convert your vehicle to use leaded fuel, you will have a problem (and you must convert it back before bringing it home). If your rig has a large gasoline engine, bear in mind that gasoline is much more expensive in the U.K. and Europe.

Most European motorhomes use diesel fuel (half the price of gasoline in Europe), or are small, economical vans. Their speedometers and odometers are calibrated in kilometers, they have European fittings for gas and electricity, and they are otherwise better suited for use on the Continent. It's much wiser to just give your local rig a rest and plan on buying and selling one over there. You can get a dependable vehicle with a buy-back guarantee from a dealer, use it as long as you want, and wind up spending less than the cost of shipping your own (which is saved a lot of wear and tear).

If, after all the foregoing negativity, you still have overriding reasons to ship your own rig across the ocean, here is a list of shipping agencies you can call:

West Coast

- Farber & Co. (Broker/Consolidator)
  444 W. Ocean Blvd. #516
  Long Beach, CA 90802
  Tel: (310) 432-8748

- H. Schumacher Associates
  1231 E. 230th St.
  Carson, CA 90745
  Tel: (310) 549-8550
  (Offices in Bremen)

East Coast

- AAACON Auto Transport, Inc.
  230 West 41st St.
  New York, NY
  Tel. (212) 354-7777

- Auto Overseas Ltd.
  New York, NY
  Tel: (212) 221-5955

Gulf Coast

- P&O Containers
  Houston, TX
  Tel: (800) 835 7447

To avoid problems (we've heard some real horror stories) call the Interstate Commerce Commission (ICC) first. They will tell you which shippers can be expected to leave your rig on the dock for more than a month, waiting to fill the container, which ones may fail to pay the freight bills, so that your rig is impounded, and which ones may send it to Montevideo by mistake.

ICC East: (215) 596-4040

ICC West: (213) 894-4008

(Courtesy Lufthansa German Airlines)

Chapter 2

Prep Talk:
Trip Planning Tips

Getting to Europe is not difficult these days. There are a few tips we can give you, however, that will help you cut some red tape, save a little money, and have an easier, more enjoyable trip.

WHEN TO GO

Europe enjoys relatively good weather from early April through late October. Some campgrounds may open later and close earlier. "High season," the heavy tourist rush, is mid-June through the end of August. The middle two weeks of August are especially crowded. We prefer to avoid this period, when prices are highest and the weather is hottest. Southern Europe can really sizzle in midsummer, but spring and fall are beautiful there. October is the golden month in Greece, Italy, southern France, Spain, Portugal, and Turkey. But Northern Europe and the British Isles can be achingly cold and damp in early spring and late fall, so you may want to plan to be there in the warmer months.

If you're interested in flowers, late April and May are worth the cold nights, especially in England and Holland.

If you're wintering over in Europe, you'll find mild weather in Crete, Sicily and southern Spain even in December. Gibraltar is popular among vanners, and many cross over to Morocco or head for Turkey. And if

Rick Steves'

EUROPE THROUGH THE BACK DOOR CATALOG

All items are field tested, discount priced (prices include tax and shipping),
completely guaranteed, and highly recommended for European travel.

CONVERTIBLE BACK DOOR BAG $75

At 9"x22"x13" our specially designed, sturdy bag is maximum carry-on-the-plane size (fits under the seat) and your key to footloose and fancy-free travel. Made of rugged water resistant cordura nylon, it converts easily from a smart looking suitcase to a handy rucksack. It has padded hide-away shoulder straps, top and side handles, and a detachable shoulder strap (for use as a suitcase). Lockable perimeter zippers allow easy access to the roomy 2,500 cubic inch central compartment. Two large outside compartments are perfect for frequently used items. A nylon stuff bag is also included. Rick Steves and over 40,000 other Back Door travelers have used these bags around the world. Available in black, grey, navy blue and teal green.

MONEYBELT $8

Absolutely required for European travel, our sturdy nylon, ultra-light, under-the-pants pouch is just big enough to carry your essentials (passport, airline tickets, travelers checks, and so on) comfortably. Rick won't travel without one, and neither should you. Comes in neutral beige, with a nylon zipper. One size fits all.

EUROPEAN RAILPASSES

We sell the full range of European railpasses, and with every Eurailpass we give you these important extras -- *free:* Rick Steves' hour-long 'How to get the most out of your railpass' video; your choice of one of Rick's seven "2 to 22 Days in..." guidebooks; and our comments on your 1-page proposed itinerary. Call us for a free copy of our *Back Door Guide to European Railpasses.*

BACK DOOR 'BEST OF EUROPE' TOURS

We offer a variety of European tours for those who want to travel in the Back Door style, but without the transportation and hotel hassles. These tours feature small groups, our own guides, Back Door accomodations, and lots of physical exercise. Our tours aren't for everyone, but they may be just the ticket for you. Call us for details.

FREE TRAVEL NEWSLETTER/CATALOG

Give us a call at (206) 771-8303, and we'll send you our free newsletter/catalog packed full of timely information on budget travel, books, maps, videos railpasses and Back Door tours. We'll help you travel better *because* you're on a budget -- not in spite of it.

Prices are good through 1994 (maybe longer), and include tax and shipping (allow
2 to 3 weeks). Sorry, no credit cards or phone orders. Send checks in US $ to:

Europe Through the Back Door ❖ **120 Fourth Avenue North**
PO Box 2009, Edmonds, WA 98020 ❖ **Phone: (206)771-8303**

you want to ski, you'll find snow in the Alps most of the year.

BOOKING YOUR FLIGHT

Your travel agent can help you choose from the many flights available from just about every major city in the known world. There are low-cost charter flights and APEX (advance purchase excursion) fares, bulk fares and "bucket shop" tickets, which you'll find advertised in the Sunday newspaper travel section. One interesting option is a Lufthansa flight that lands in Frankfurt, then treats you to a scenic train ride up the Rhine.

If you have lots of time, you might want to float across the Atlantic on a freighter, a cruise ship, or a yacht.

However you choose to go, pay for your ticket with a credit card. You'll get free flight insurance with some cards, and you'll be much more sure to get what you paid for than if you had forked over cash or a check. With a credit card, you have the right to dispute the bill if necessary.

IMPORTANT PAPERS

PASSPORT

You need a passport to travel outside your home country. The airline will ask to see it before they let you on the plane. In the U.S., you can apply for a passport at certain post office locations in major cities, at courthouses in some locations, and at passport agencies. In Canada, you can go to a passport office or apply by mail to Ottawa.

VISAS

You will need visas to enter some countries. These requirements change from time to time. For current visa information call Visas International at (800) 638-1517.

INTERNATIONAL DRIVING PERMIT

This document is highly overrated. It is said to be necessary for driving in Europe, and it does provide translations of your driver's license into several different languages, but whenever we've presented ours to a police officer in Europe, we've been asked for our U.S. state license instead. It's a good thing to have in eastern Europe, however. And at some campgrounds, it can be used as official identification in lieu of your passport, and you won't be inconvenienced by its loss. It is available from the American Automobile Association (AAA), the National Automobile Club (NAC), and the Canadian Automobile Association (CAA).

INTERNATIONAL CAMPING CARNET

This is a valuable document. In fact, it is required at most campgrounds in London, Paris, and Denmark. It identifies you as a "serious" camping person and gets you more respect at campgrounds. It also gets you a discount at some, and is accepted at most in lieu of your passport (which you normally must surrender during your stay to insure payment. This is not a good idea for you because legally you must carry your passport at all times).

The carnet is available in the U.S. from:

- National Campers & Hikers Association, Inc.
  4804 Transit Road, Bldg. 2
  Depew, NY 14043-4704
  Tel. (716) 668-6242

or in Canada from:

- National Campers & Hikers Association
  51 W. 22nd St.
  Hamilton, Ontario L9C 4N5
  Tel. (416) 385-1866

You must join NCHA for $20.00, after which you may buy the carnet for $10.00. You can also buy a carnet in Europe for less than $10 at auto club offices, some campgrounds, or the International Federation of Camping and Caravanning (FICC), Rue de Rivoli, Paris. One per family is sufficient.

CHANGING MONEY

It's a good idea to buy traveler's cheques in German Marks, the most stable currency in Europe. Thomas Cook offices sell them commission-free, and they are cashed free in the local currency at TC offices and many banks in Europe. Exchange the leftovers for your home currency in Europe (preferably in Germany) before you leave. If necessary, use credit cards for cash advances (extra fees are usually charged for these transactions, and of course, interest accrues from day one).

WHAT TO TAKE

One of the more pleasant advantages of traveling by

van or motorhome is that there's no need to pack and unpack every day. No more will you have to fold each thing just right, decide which suitcase to put it in and then remember it, sit on your luggage and try to tuck in all the loose ends just to get it closed, and lug it up and down hotel steps every day.

On this trip you'll need to pack only twice: when you leave home and when you leave Europe. Between those times you can relax and spread out and surround yourself with the things you choose. Don't choose too many things, though; you want to be able to put everything out of the way in cupboards. It's a good idea to pack two days before your trip, in case you forget something.

CLOTHES

Most vans and motorhomes have at least one closet where you can hang dresses, sport coats, etc., but space is limited. Still, you won't need a lot of elaborate outfits, so it's best to keep it simple. Bring mostly soft clothes that you can fold into the variously shaped storage compartments. Remember also to bring only soft suitcases, which can be folded up and stowed out of the way.

A well-broken-in pair of comfortable walking shoes with thick waterproof soles is the most important item in your travel wardrobe. A warm jacket comes next. Think more about comfort and durability than looking spiffy. Dark colors and prints last longer between launderings; leave those white pants and pale blouses at home. In most European cities nice jeans and sweatshirts are perfectly acceptable streetwear for both sexes. You'll need one dressy outfit for the occasional elegant restaurant or evening at the theater, but otherwise casual wear is more appropriate. And an additional tip: don't bring t-shirts and blouses with shoulder pads.

They take too long to dry in the laundry or on the clothes line.

CLOTHES PACKING CHECKLIST

There are some items of clothing that we consider indispensable. You will surely have some additions and deletions, but this list will help you make sure you don't forget anything important:

- Jeans or other sturdy pants
- No-iron sport shirts (men)
- No-iron blouses (women)
- T-shirts
- Warm sweater or sweatshirt
- Water-repellent jacket
- Shorts (but not too short)
- Cool tops (women)
- Swimsuits (two-piece for topless beaches)
- Comfortable walking shoes and sandals
- Plastic sandals (for showers and rocky beaches)
- Sport coat, dress shirt and tie (men)
- One nice skirt and top or dress (women)
- Dress shoes and socks or stockings
- Thermal underwear for fall and winter

MOTORING NEEDS

You will be driving a lot on this trip, so why not make the experience as pleasant and enjoyable as possible? Here are a few items that you can take along to make your roads smoother, little things that you may not normally consider necessary for your daily driving.

- Maps - or get them in Europe
- Tool Kit - metric wrenches, pliers, screwdrivers
- Aerosol tire inflator - just in case
- Sunglasses - for the increased glare of European light

- Binoculars - for castles, birds, and reading street signs
- Compass - helps you orient yourself in cities
- Driving gloves - for cold mountain driving
- Flashlight - and be sure the batteries are fresh

HEALTH NEEDS

We'll talk more about health in chapter nine, but you're packing right now, so we'll give you this list right here. You can buy most of these items in Western Europe, but if you already have them, it's easier to pack them. And when you're hurting, you're not in the mood to figure out what they call your chosen form of relief in Hungarian:

- Aspirin or other analgesic
- Antihistamines, antacid, laxatives, etc.
- Band-aids
- Medication you use often (bring copies of prescriptions written as generics, since the trade names can differ)
- Eyeglasses (spare pair or copy of prescription)
- Contact lenses (spare pair, supplies, prescription)
- Vitamins (if you usually take them)
- Favorite soaps, shampoos, toiletries

FUN AND COMFORT ITEMS

These are the little luxuries that will make your trip easier and more enjoyable. Some of them will make you feel more at home, some will have a practical use, and others will just add to your fun:

- Folding umbrella
- Small calculator
- Address book, notebook
- Favorite sporting equipment

- Business cards
- Travel sewing kit, including small scissors
- Light nylon day pack
- Cameras and film (more expensive in Europe)
- A few zip-lock bags for different currencies
- Small, light shaving or cosmetic kit with hanging strap
- About six feet of clothesline and some clothespins

And if you're planning to buy, not rent, your van or motorhome:

- Favorite wine glasses, coffee cups, dishes, table ware
- Towels, bedding (or buy at flea markets and stores when you arrive)

DOCUMENT CHECKLIST

Some of these were mentioned above, but this check-list will help you make sure you have them all. You *can't* leave home without some of them, while others will make it a lot easier:

- Passport
- Plane tickets
- Auto club card
- Credit cards (check expiration dates)
- Optical prescription
- Driver's license and International Driver's License
- Traveler's cheques
- Guidebooks
- Medical insurance claim forms (if needed)
- Camping carnet
- Phrase books

Chapter 3

Roads And Driving
Breezing Along Like a Native

Driving in Europe is a good part of the adventure. Exploring on your own is much more exciting than leaving the driving to others. The total freedom of going and stopping wherever your wanderlust takes you is an important ingredient of a satisfying experience. You'll enjoy the sweeping view from your high vantage point, surveying the countryside over the roofs of most other vehicles. You'll appreciate the added safety of that view, too. And traffic jams are much more bearable when you can have cheese and crackers while you wait.

THE ROADS

Europe is criss-crossed by a very good international network of limited-access highways. The British generic term for this type of road is *motorway*, and that's the one we'll use.

There are also many two-lane primary and secondary roads that wind through the countryside. These roads take you past Roman ruins, medieval castles, quaint farmhouses, and intriguing places to shop. They are slower than motorways, of course, but much more interesting.

MOTORWAYS
These are divided highways, with on-ramps and off-ramps, normally with two lanes each way in the country

and more in the city. They're almost identical to the freeways and expressways you're used to at home. The passing lane is on the left (right in Great Britain), and drivers are very scrupulous about using it only when overtaking a slower vehicle. Some drivers go much faster than others on these roads, and they demand a clear passing lane. You needn't feel pressured to drive any faster than you deem best, as long as you stay in the "slow" lane.

MOTORWAY ETIQUETTE

Drivers throughout Europe follow the same general set of rules and customs, and you'll be expected to conform. A driver who wants you to move over so that he can pass will come up to a respectable distance behind you and flash his left (right in G.B.) turn signal. If you don't notice him and signal that you're getting out of his way, he'll probably come closer to your back bumper and put two wheels over on the shoulder to emphasize his urgent need and properly fill your mirrors. If you still don't respond he will flash his headlights. Horn-honking is an extreme last resort on European highways.

When you wish to overtake a slower vehicle, check your mirrors carefully for for a clear gap in the passing lane. Judge the speed of the next car approaching behind, flash your left turn signal, get out there and go as fast as you can. As soon as it's safe, signal right and get back in the right lane. Drivers will not curse you and shake their fists as they sometimes do at home.

In fact, motorhomes are expected to go slowly, and it's wise to limit your speed to 100 kph (62 mph) unless the limit is lower. Cruising at this speed or slower, you will reap substantial benefits in increased fuel economy, decreased wear and tear on the machinery, and increased safety. In addition, you'll be more relaxed, you'll be better able to hear the stereo and each other, and the scenery won't go by in a blur. You've come to <u>see</u> Europe, not just get through it, and there's plenty to see, even from the motorway.

Germany

This country has the largest number of motorways, and they are all toll-free. They are called *autobahn,* and most of them have no speed limit unless weather conditions dictate. Don't be alarmed, therefore, if while cruising along at a respectable speed you catch a flash of quartz-halogen light in your mirror, hear a great *whoosh!*, and suddenly find yourself watching the tail end of a Mercedes or BMW disappearing over the horizon

---

THE TOURIST ATTRACTION FROM HELL

It has become Germany's answer to the Eiffel Tower, the adopted symbol of Disneyland, and a huge tourist draw. It's on the cover of this book. But Neuschwanstein, mad King Ludwig's 19th-century fantasy of a medieval fairytale castle, is The Tourist Attraction From Hell.

After being deterred by the crowds during the tourist season, we tried again in October. We paid the exorbitant parking fee, then made the steep half-hour climb to the castle gate. There we bought expensive admission tickets and got in line. We counted 300 people between us and the door, which we reached in about 40 minutes. Then the line shuffled through the first gift shop. We hadn't seen anything yet.

To make a very long story short, we spent nearly two hours trapped in line, unable to go backward or forward, reading graffiti left on the walls by other bored tourists. Then we were rushed through six rooms and out into another gift shop in 25 minutes flat by a fast-talking guide.

In tourist season, the wait begins on the road, miles before you reach the parking lot. Good Luck!

at twice your velocity. For the situations where there are speed limits, the police drive Porsches just to keep up.

France

French motorways are called *autoroute,* and many of them are designated *peage* (pronounced pay-*azh*), because you must pay to drive on them. They're worth it, though; they are some of the best roads in Europe: smooth, well-maintained, and quite scenic for motorways. They also boast the best services; filling stations, restaurants, grocery and gift shops, luxury hotels and even night clubs are right there in the service areas. But the best part for us is the beautiful rest areas, or *aires,* where people in vans, motorhomes, and trailers can park free and enjoy a peaceful night's sleep among the trees.

But beware! Many *autoroutes* have automatic toll booths. When entering them you are expected to push a big red button (sometimes high, sometimes low) and take a ticket, even if there is no attendant watching. If you neglect to do this and have no ticket when you reach the exit booth, you will be charged the maximum toll, which can be as much as thirty or forty dollars. Major credit cards are accepted from those who make this expensive mistake and plead lack of cash.

Italy

Autostrada is the Italian word for motorway. Most of them are toll roads and they're the most expensive in Europe. They're also the most necessary; the alternative is a network of narrow, winding farm roads that merely connect villages instead of proceeding in any one direction. A trip that takes hours on the *autostrada* can take days on the back roads.

Austria

Austria's motorways are mostly free, the exceptions being Alpine roads and tunnels. These were built with great difficulty and at great cost, and the high tolls are quite understandable. They save a lot of difficult, time-consuming driving through mountains that are otherwise impassable at times.

Switzerland

The efficient Swiss don't bother to maintain toll booths on individual roads, except for a few motorways and tunnels. They simply charge you a flat fee (about 30 Swiss Francs for a one-year sticker) at the border. Consider it as admission to the world's largest theme park.

Great Britain

The motorways of England, Northern Ireland, and Scotland are toll-free, well-maintained, scenic, and quite pleasant to drive on. They are quite different, however, from those on the Continent in that you must drive on the opposite side of the road. Keeping left is not so difficult on the divided motorway, but you should remember that here the fast lane is on the right and exit ramps are on the left. Getting used to this usually doesn't take very long.

Spain

The *autopista* that runs down along the Costa Brava, Spain's Mediterranean coast, saves time but there is a lot of tourist development and traffic congestion along that stretch. It's a continuation of the E4 from France, and it takes you across the Pyrenees, through Barcelona and all the way down to Alicante. The tolls are modest and can be paid by credit card. Another *autopista* skirts the industrial cities of the north coast. Otherwise, Spain's primary highways are among the best anywhere. They are wide, smooth, scenic, and lightly-traveled. *Autovias* are non-toll motorways, usually found around cities.

Greece

Highway 1 is a toll road that winds from the Macedonian border all the way down to Athens. It snakes along the rocky coastline and through forested mountains and is very scenic. It's not a divided motorway but a two-lane highway with wide shoulders that slower vehicles are obliged to use when faster ones want to pass. Until you've driven it, you haven't seen Greece. It's worth the modest toll.

Czech Republic

There are some motorways here, but it's mostly two-lane blacktop, quite satisfactory for the gentle traffic outside Prague. There are no tolls.

Hungary

No tolls here, either. Motorways serve the heaviest traffic areas, but two-lanes predominate.

With few exceptions, motorways in all the other European countries are free. Some countries have no motorways at all, and some have very few.

The Netherlands still honors its seafaring traditions and watery foundations by stopping all four lanes of high-speed traffic on the main east-west motorway, or *snelweg,* to raise its drawbridge whenever a boat skipper wishes to glide serenely through on the canal beneath. Sometimes several skippers wish to glide serenely through, and long lines of traffic build up in either direction. But the wait is relatively short, and the experience gives one a taste of the Dutch personality.

MOTORWAY SERVICES

Europe's motorways could be called "self-contained." One could drive for hundreds of kilometers, indeed through several countries, without ever leaving the motorway. There is no need to waste travel time searching for places to eat, sleep, shop or even to have your vehicle repaired. Along the motorways there are large rest/service areas which include filling stations, repair shops, and stores where auto parts and accessories, souvenirs, gifts, snack foods, maps, and local wines can be bought. There are restaurants, bars, and motels, and large, often nicely landscaped parking areas where you can sleep in your motorhome in quiet and safety.
The best of these are in France, as mentioned above, but many countries have them.

There are also smaller rest areas located more frequently along the motorways, marked by a "P" sign. In some countries, these are equipped with restrooms, picnic tables, and other amenities. They are usually out in the country, and often include patches of forest, wildflower-studded meadows, and breathtaking views. They can be very pleasant places to stop for a short break, a picnic lunch, or dinner and a good night's rest.

These features make Europe's motorway system a world unto itself, with only one caveat: distances between those refueling stops can be long. Make sure you have enough fuel to make it comfortably to the next one.

CROSSING BORDERS

Borders used to be places to be approached with trepidation. You combed your hair and tidied up beforehand, rehearsed saying "Good Morning, sir" in the new country's language, and got butterflies in your stomach when you handed your passport to the tight-lipped official. Nowadays, with the increased communication and cooperation between Western European countries as a result of the European Community (EC) and liberalization in much of Eastern Europe, many border stations have become ghost towns where the money exchange and duty-free shop are the only remaining signs of life and traffic sails by unimpeded. Often these days we find ourselves looking for subtle clues, like the language on highway signs and the architecture of houses, to ascertain that we have indeed crossed the border. (EC countries post little blue signs with the EC flag and stars before the border, but they're easy to miss, and spoil the game.)

These subtle differences, including changes in the landscape and vegetation, road surface and markings, town names and prevalent license plates, add another facet to your travel experience. They show why the boundary between countries and cultures is where it is.

DON'T CROSS AT NIGHT

For that reason and others that we'll cover below, it's not a good idea to cross borders at night. Find a place to sleep and cross in the morning. Usually there are large free parking lots at borders for just this purpose, but trucks pull in and out of them all night long and they're not very quiet. It's much better to find a campground or a roadside "P" to spend the night before you cross. Here's why:

1. Changing Money

Until the EC adopts a single currency, you are help-
less without the proper money if you come upon a toll
booth, if you want to stop for coffee or dinner at a restaurant, or if you need fuel. Credit cards are not accepted for
these things in many places. You should always change
money immediately after crossing into a new country,
but not at the border exchange booth. You will get a
much more favorable rate at a bank in the first town you
come to.

Clean out your pockets and put away your leftover
money of the country you're leaving to avoid confusion. If
you're not coming back, you can change the paper money,
but not the coins, or buy fuel with it before you cross the
border. Remember, every time you change from one currency to another, you lose money. Some currencies
(Greek, Portuguese, and Eastern European monies, for
example) are nearly worthless outside their home countries.

2. Culture Shock

Switching languages and cultures takes energy, and
it's a shock to your system. At the end of a long, adven-
ture-filled day, everything is more difficult. Finding a
place to sleep in the dark, especially if you're looking for
a specific campground, can be a nightmare. Most important, you should avoid arriving in a new country by ferry
after dark unless you are sure that you can finish out the
night by sleeping at the dock. Otherwise, you will be
directed by impatient traffic wardens (and swept along
in a stream of cars and trucks) out into the maze of the
city. If you napped during the ferry crossing, you will be
disoriented and very grumpy.

3. Missing Scenery

As we mentioned earlier, it's part of the adventure to note the changes in topography and culture that caused the border to be put there in the first place,. Unless you're pressed for time, we don't recommend driving at night at all. Apart from safety considerations, think of all the scenery you're missing.

SOME BORDERS STILL GUARDED

While many borders are easily passed, some are not. Greece, for instance, still suffers age-old tensions with her neighbors, Turkey and Macedonia, and border guards of all three countries act accordingly. Expect a few questions and possibly a brief search when crossing between these countries. Entering Portugal involves filling out forms, but no searches or other unpleasantries. Austria maintains the long waiting line tradition, and many Eastern European borders still require a check of passports, visas and entry permits.

Highway signs in some countries will often show only the name of the border town on their side, but not the sometimes larger one across the border. Note this when checking the map for directions.

ASKING DIRECTIONS

Asking directions is an important skill to have whenever you're out of your home neighborhood. Don't laugh; all the map-reading, compass-pointing, odometer-counting, sun-looking, head-scratching, rigmate-arguing, and second-guessing won't tell you what the filling station attendant knows: that construction crews on the road ahead have tied up traffic, but that there's another, more scenic road a few kilometers north. And there's a three-star restaurant on the way.

And of course, that attendant is delighted to be able to help somebody with his bit of knowledge. He may ask you some questions, too, and you'll both have a pleasant experience understanding a bit more about each other's culture.

THE DRIVER-NAVIGATOR RELATIONSHIP

It takes two. The navigator studies the maps, discusses the alternatives with the driver, then figures out the best route to take, keeps track of mileage, and gets the change ready for toll booths. The navigator tells the driver ahead of time what signs to look for and what to do when they appear.

The driver drives.

A good tip for sign-looking is to notice on the map the names of towns and other landmarks near where you want to go. Your specific destination may not be on the sign, but you'll know which way to turn if you recognize its neighbor.

A useful navigator service anywhere in the world is to look right (left in Great Britain) at intersections and tell the driver whether or not it's safe to pull out. Most vans and motorhomes have a blind spot on the right, and entering intersections is much safer this way. The navigator says "Okay Right" when it's clear, and "Wait!" when it's not.

Driver-navigator teamwork is healthy for a relationship. The driver learns to trust the navigator's judgment, and the navigator becomes a necessary part of the travel process, not just a passenger. And it keeps them both from getting lost. But finding your way around in foreign countries can be stressful, so it is essential to agree that anything said in the heat of navigation doesn't count.

CITY DRIVING

Driving in European cities is not as easy as it used to be, It was always a challenge, squeezing through narrow winding, cobbled medieval streets while several hot-blooded would-be Grand Prix drivers competed for your position. But now it seems that every European has a car and urban traffic is often in a frustrating snarl. Audacious young riders of mufflerless mopeds buzz around you like gnats. It's not the best way to go sightseeing.

The notion that you can drive around the block and return to the same place dies hard in New-World drivers, us included. We still try it once in a while, but it seldom works out. The centers of *our* cities, for the most part, were laid out all at once by engineers and surveyors on a square grid. Main Street intersects with First, then Second, and so on. In Europe, however, most cities grew up randomly around the nucleus of a castle or a port. To confuse invaders, nobody was eager to make it easy to find a way through the maze. People walked where the cattle had made a path, and these paths later became streets. So the inner grids of most European cities were planned by cows and sheep, who are not too good at geometry.

HOW TO GET AROUND IN A NEW TOWN

When you approach a city, first look for the signs leading to the central area. Most are variations on the word "center", such as *Centrum, Centro, Centre Ville, Zentrum,* or something similar. In many German cities the word is *Stadtmitte.*

Follow these signs and soon you will see arrows pointing to the *Tourist Bureau.* This term, too, comes in variations, but it's almost always recognizable (or even in English).

One major exception is France, where the Tourist Bureau is called the *Syndicat d'Initiative* or *Office du Tourisme*. Another is the Netherlands, where you should look for an inverted pyramid-shaped sign marking the VVV. Other signs used for this type of office in Europe are the "*i*" for information and a simple"*?*."

At the Tourist Bureau you can get city maps, guides to attractions and restaurants, and information about such things as campgrounds, laundries, supermarkets, swimming pools, and public baths. All this is given cheerfully and without charge, usually in English.

Once you've had all your questions answered and you've figured out just where you want to go in town, drive your rig there, park it, and walk. You can see much more at that pace. In fact, walking around with a street map and a compass is a great way to really enjoy a city. It allows you to step into shops, stop and read interesting signs and posters, photograph things, and inspect weird foreign cars and architectural features at point-blank range.

The Best Plan

The safest and most relaxing plan for enjoying European cities is to leave your rig at the campground and take public transportation into town. In many large cities those narrow, winding inner cowpaths have been turned into walking streets, making the central city a large shopping mall, closed to vehicular traffic. The original architecture is usually preserved, and walking through these picturesque cobbled passages can be fascinating.

Roundabouts

Drivers not used to these things may find them disconcerting, if not downright hair-raising. Roundabouts are those circular intersections where everyone has to join a revolving flow, whether or not they want to turn. Then each player must find the appropriate street and exit onto it before it whizzes past. England has the most roundabouts, and the French are quite fond of them, too. You'll find a few more in other countries.

Here's how to get through a roundabout safely and pointed in the right direction:

When approaching the roundabout you often need not stop, but you must yield to vehicles already in the circular flow. When it's clear, you pull out, joining the flow (clockwise in Great Britain, counterclockwise on the Continent). It's best to stay at the outer edge of this merry-go-round, so that you can jump off safely when you suddenly find that you've come around to the street you want to be on. The navigator must figure out which street to turn onto and tell the driver, who is busy avoiding other vehicles. Driving and reading signs in a foreign language is a two-person job.

If you miss your turn, no problem; just go around again and catch it next time.

Finding Fuel

Filling stations are easy to find in the countryside; there are frequent signs on the motorways indicating the distance to the next service area, using international symbols for the various services available, such as gasoline, diesel, LPG, restaurants, lodging, restrooms, and shops.

But in many cities finding the fuel of your choice can be tricky at first. Filling stations are not on every street corner. They are usually found outside the central city, in the suburbs and near the motorways. France is an exception here, too; curbside pumps abound in French cities. In other countries, some oil companies provide directories to their stations.

Tho boot way to find one, howevei, is to ask. Here is a list of the words that will get you refueled in the major languages of Europe:

- North American: *Gasoline* (gas-o-*leen*)
- British: *Petrol* (*pet*-roll)
- Dutch: *Petrol* (*pet*-roll)
- French: *Essence* (es-*sahns*)
- German: *Benzin* (ben-*seen*)
- Greek: *Venzine* (ven-*zee*-na)
- Portuguese: *Gasolina* (gahs-o-*lee*-na)
- Scandinavian: *Bensin* (*ben*-soon)
- Spanish: *Gasolina* (gahs-o-*lee*-na)

The German "Benzin" works throughout eastern Europe. Asking for "gas" will only get you fuel for your propane stove.

When you get to the filling station, you will have a choice to make. Leaded regular gas is called *regular* (reg-oo-*lar*) or *normal* (nor-*mahl*). Leaded super is called *super* (soo-*pair*). If you need unleaded fuel, just look for the pump with the green stripe. Diesel is usually called *Gasoleo, Gazole,* or a variation thereof, if not *Diesel*. LPG is sometimes called *autogas* or *Gepel,* and always has its own separate island.

These motorway filling stations may be convenient and enticing with their array of shops and services, but if you have time and want to save money, get off at a town and drive along the primary highway (usually parallel to the motorway) until you come to a station. You'll find the prices significantly lower in some countries, including France, Germany, Holland, and Belgium. In other countries, i.e. Italy, Spain, and all of Eastern Europe, this maneuver is unnecessary because prices are government-regulated and uniform nationwide.

That primary highway will often lead you to a *hypermarche*, a huge supermarket that sells everything, including gasoline, diesel, and automotive services. Look for big signs with names like *Mammouth* in France, *Spar* in Germany, and *Mamoet* in Holland. You will save enough on one tankful to buy a bottle of good wine. You can use major credit cards to buy fuel at many stations (except in Spain and Austria), but not your gasoline credit card from home. The sign on the station may look the same, but the system is different in most cases.

HELP ON THE ROAD

A good low-cost insurance against highway problems like breakdowns, flat tires, or running out of fuel is membership in an auto club, like the American Automobile Association (AAA), or National Automobile Club (NAC) in the U.S., the Canadian Automobile Association (CAA) in Canada, or the Automobile Association (AA) in Great Britain, Australia, or New Zealand.

These organizations have reciprocal agreements with most major European auto clubs, which will honor your club's card and provide "breakdown service," though not always free. Most clubs have service cars patrolling the major highways, and many countries have call boxes along the roadsides for summoning help. If neither is available, you can use the nearest telephone to look up the local office of the auto club serving the country you're in. They're listed below. Usually there is an English-speaking operator to take your call.

If no directory is available and the helpful people you meet don't speak English, point to the name of the club on the list below. They'll get the idea and find the nearest office for you. Or you can call the national emergency assistance number on the list at the end of this chapter.

The following clubs have reciprocal agreements with the AA, AAA, CAA and NAC, and will provide emergency road service, often at no charge to members:

Austria
* Österreichischer Automobil-Motorrad-und-Touring Club (ÖAMTC)

Belgium
* Royal Automobile Club du Belgique

Bulgaria
* Union of Bulgarian Motorists

Czech Republic
* Ulstredni Automoto Club (CSFR)

Denmark
* Forenede Dansk Motorejere (FDM)

Finland
* Finnish Automobile and Touring Club

France
* Automobile Club National (ACN)

Germany
- Allgemeiner Deutscher Automobil-Club e.V. (ADAC)

Great Britain
- The Automobile Association (AA)

Greece
- Automobile and Touring Club of Greece (ELPA)

Hungary
- Magyar Auto Club (MAC)

Italy
- Automobile Club d'Italia (ACI)

Luxembourg
- Automobile Club du Grande Duche de Luxembourg (ACL)

Netherlands
- Koninklijke Nederlandse Toeristenbond (ANWB)

Norway
- Norges Automobil-Forbund (NAF)

Poland
- Polski Zwiazek Motorowi (PZM)

Portugal
- Automivel Club do Portugal (ACP)

Romania
- Rumanischer Auto Club (RAC)

Switzerland
- Touring Club Suisse (TCS)

Turkey
- Turkiye Touring ve Otomobil Kuruma (TTOK)

In countries not listed, don't count on free help from the local auto club. They may help you and charge you for it, or call an independent breakdown service. If you must make direct payment, get a receipt; your home club may reimburse you. If you're driving a rented vehicle, the rental company should reimburse you, or they may pay directly.

HIGHWAY SIGNS

Because of the many different languages spoken in Europe and the mobility of its citizens, road signs have been standardized in an international picture language. Many are self-explanatory. Others are not so easy to figure out. Here are the most important signs and what they're trying to tell you:

INTERNATIONAL ROAD SIGNS

 NARROWING ROAD

 MEN AT WORK

 CURVES

 TRAFFIC LIGHT AHEAD

 ROUGH ROAD

 CROSSROADS

 SCHOOL CROSSING

 DANGEROUS CROSSROAD

 PEDESTRIAN CROSSING

 ROAD JUNCTION

 FALLING ROCKS

 RAILROAD CROSSING

 NO ENTRY

 NO U TURN

 ROAD CLOSED

 NO PASSING

 DO NOT ENTER

 QUIET ZONE

 NO TURN IN DIRECTION INDICATED

 SPEED LIMIT

Roads & Driving

PARKING AND NO-PARKING SIGNS

No Stopping

NIFT
PARKEREN

Parking Prohibited

ESTATIONMENT
INTERDIT

Closed to all Vehicles

P

Parking Allowed

On nearly every road and in nearly every city and town in Europe you will find legal parking spaces under the blue "P" sign (pictured above). In built-up areas these may be paid parking lots, but out in the country they are almost always free. They are described fully in the "Sleeping" chapter.

There are also many places in Europe where you may *not* park. Most are marked by the international signs (pictured above). More specific ones, found mostly along the French and Italian Rivieras, depict a trailer or motorhome with the familiar "no-no" slash drawn over it, or a motorhome being towed away. While we have never seen these signs enforced outside of high season, we do not recommend your testing them.

MAPS AND GUIDEBOOKS

No matter how freely you want to wander, it's good to know where you are once in a while. Accurate maps and sound guidebooks will help you choose the places you want to go and the things you want to see, as well as the most direct, quickest, most scenic, or most toll-free way to get there.

You'll need, first of all, an overall map of the Continent. Your local AAA, AA, CAA, or NAC office can provide a planning map that shows major highways, cities and towns, borders, distances, toll roads, and ferries to help you decide where it's possible, practical, desirable, and advisable to go. Auto club offices also have assorted guidebooks which you may find helpful. There is a charge, in most cases, for maps and guidebooks, but they are available to non-members as well as members.

The most detailed maps come from Europe itself, and can be found in travel bookstores. They're also available in Europe, of course, at bookstores, newsstands, and filling stations.

Auto club members can get very good maps, guidebooks, and other publications at offices of affiliated clubs in Europe. In most cases, all publications are in the language of the issuing club's country. Most publications are free of charge to affiliated club members; others are sold at member discount rates. For a list of European auto clubs with reciprocal agreements with U.S. and Canadian clubs, see "HELP ON THE ROAD" (above).

FERRIES

A comprehensive listing of European ferries with their addresses and frequencies (but not schedules and prices) can be found in the back of the Europa Campground Guide. A good general rule to follow is that if there is more than one route to a place, the longer ride will be cheaper.

THE ENGLISH CHANNEL

In the Eurotunnel, a train whisks you and your van from Calais, France to Folkestone, England in one hour (incl. loading and unloading) for about the same cost as a ferry ride. There are several different ferry lines making the crossing several times a day, and different routes ranging in time from one hour (by hovercraft) to 36 hours (from Norway). The shortest crossing is between Dover, England and Calais. The fastest conventional boat takes 75 minutes. Choices of lines, routes, sailing times, and rates are infinite, and each line publishes voluminous schedules listing them. The rates range from "A" (highest) to "E" (lowest).

The Best Ferry Deal

The best deal we've found is on the Sally Line, which sails between Ramsgate, England (near Dover) and Dunkerque, France (near Calais). This trip takes 150 minutes, but Sally offers lower "E" rates (offered only at certain times on certain days), and more of them. Another big advantage is Sally's large terminal parking lots at both ports where motorhomers and caravanners are welcome to spend the night before or after sailing. It's an impromptu free campground, with toilets, washing facilities, a small restaurant in the terminal, and lots of friendly people to share travel stories with. Other ferry ports are too crowded and busy for this sort of thing. And we found the Sally people pleasant, the boats clean and well-appointed, and the food quite good on board, all of which are exceptions to the general rule.

The Best Time

The best time to cross the Channel is at 8:30 a.m. on a Monday, Tuesday, or Wednesday. The fares are cheapest then, and you can sleep at the terminal, wake up and get on the boat (ask a neighbor to knock in the morning), and arrive with most of the day still ahead. "E" rate applies only to vehicles up to 5.5 meters (214 inches) in length; there is an extra charge per meter beyond that. Consult current schedules for prices.

Other Ferries

Other ferries sail regularly between many other countries in Europe and the British Isles. Consult local schedules for their sailing times and rates.

You can take your vehicle to the Greek Islands and save more than the cost of the ferry ride. You won't need a hotel or a rental car, and although there are very few formal campgrounds, you can freecamp just about anywhere. Samos, one of the most beautiful islands, is a stone's throw from Turkey. But the ferry, a bouncing bathtub toy with room for three cars on the afterdeck (you must drive aboard on two undulating wooden planks, then back down them to get ashore), is criminally expensive and should be avoided. Go from Samos to Rhodes, and then on to Turkey.

Most ferries are large and very stable, with shops, restaurants, lounges and staterooms on board. Nearly all prohibit staying in your vehicle while underway; you must leave it and ride up on the passenger decks. As you approach your destination, loudspeakers will ask all drivers to go below and get ready to exit as soon as the boat docks.

NATIONAL HIGHWAY LAWS and EMERGENCY ASSISTANCE TELEPHONE NUMBERS

In general, campers and motorhomes up to 3.5 tons are subject to the same laws and speed limits that govern passenger cars. Vehicles over 3.5 tons and cars with trailers are subject to lower speed limits and size restrictions. Seatbelts are required in every country except Italy. Speed limits are expressed in kilometers per hour (km, km/h or kph), except in Great Britain, where they still use miles. To convert km to miles, multiply by .62. 100 km/h = 62 mph, 80 km/h = 49 mph, etc. Emergency numbers will connect you with the police.

Austria
* Speed limits: main roads 100, motorways 130.
  Over 3.5T: 60/70. Emergency: tel. 144.

Belgium
* Speed limits: main roads 90, motorways 120.
  Over 3.5T: 60/90. Emergency: tel. 100.

Commonwealth of Independent States (CIS)
* Speed limits: main roads 110, motorways 110.
  Over 3.5T: 70/70. Emergency: tel. 03.
  Visa req., procured in advance. No night driving.

Croatia, Kosmet, Macedonia, Montenegro, Serbia, Slovenia

- Speed limits: main roads 80, motorways 120.
  Over 3.5T: 70/80. Emergency: tel. 94.
  Travel vouchers required 30 days in advance.

Bulgaria

- Speed limits: main roads 80, motorways 120.
  Over 3.5T: 70/80. Emergency: tel. 146.
  Tourist coupons required to purchase motor fuel.

Czech Republic

- Speed limits: main roads 90, motorways 110.
  Over 3.5T: 80/80. Emergency: tel. 155.

Denmark

- Speed limits: main roads 80, motorways 100.
  Over 3.5T: 60/80. Emergency: tel. 000.

Finland

- Speed limits: main roads 80, motorways 120.
  Over 3.5T: 80/80. Emergency: tel. 000, 005.
  Low-beam headlights required in daytime outside built-up areas.

France

- Speed limits: main roads 90, motorways 130.
  Over 3.5T: 80/100. Emergency: tel. 17.

Germany

- Speed limits: main roads 100, motorways none unless posted. Over 2.8T: 80/80. Over 2.8T: 80/80. Emergency: tel. 110.

Roads & Driving

Great Britain
- Speed limits: main roads 60 mph (97kph), motorways 70 mph (112 kph). Over 10T: 50 mph (80 kph)/50 (80). Emergency: tel. 999.
  Drive on the Left.

Greece
- Speed limits: main roads 80, motorways 100. Over 3.5T: 70/70. Emergency: tel. 104,166.

Hungary
- Speed limits: main roads 80, motorways 120. Over 3.5T: 70/80. Emergency: tel. 04, 004.

Italy
- Speed limits: main roads 90, motorways 110/130. Over 8T: 60/80. Emergency: tel. 113.

Liechtenstein
- Speed limits: main roads 80, motorways 120. Over 3.5T: 80/80. Emergency: tel. 144.

Luxembourg
- Speed limits: main roads 90, motorways 120. Over 3.5T: 75/90. Emergency: tel. 012.

Netherlands
- Speed limits: main roads 80, motorways 120. Over 3.5T: 80/80. Emergency: tel. 0611.

Norway
- Speed limits: main roads 80, motorways 90. Over 3.5T: 80/80. Emergency: tel. 002.
  Low-beam headlights required in daytime outside

built-up areas. Smoking at the wheel forbidden in built-up areas.

Poland
- Speed limits: main roads 90, motorways 110. Over 3.5T: 70/70. Emergency: tel. 999.

Portugal
- Speed limits: main roads 90, motorways 120. Over 3.5T: 80/100. Emergency: tel. 115.

Romania
- Speed limits: main roads 80, motorways 90. Over 2.8T: 70,70. Emergency: tel. 061. Visa required; obtainable at border or in advance.

Spain
- Speed limits: main roads 90, motorways 120. Over 3.5T: 70/100. Emergency: tel. 091.

Sweden
- Speed limits: main roads 90, motorways 110. Over 3.5T: 70/90. Emergency: tel. 90000. Low-beam headlights required in daytime.

Turkey
- Speed limits: main roads 80, motorways 80. Over 3.5T: 80/80s. Emergency: tel. 077.. Two warning triangles required.

Note: Alcohol is forbidden while driving in eastern European countries, Greece, and Norway. Other European countries have much lower legal limits than the U.S. or Canada.

Chapter 4

Sleeping in the Best Places:
Nightly Homesites

CAMPGROUNDS

Now that you're on the road with your new motorhome, where are you going to stay when it gets dark? Campgrounds are easily found in Europe, and they are nearly always clean and pleasant. But the orientation is different from the North American idea of what camping is all about, and this takes some explanation.

At home when we go camping, in the back of our heads is some sort of idea of returning to our pioneer heritage. We like to go off in the wilds (or pretend we're off in the wilds) and build a bonfire for roasting hot dogs and marshmallows. We like to scare ourselves at night with stories of bears and snakes, and we like to think that we're roughing it. Consequently our campgrounds tend to be way off in the wilderness and the individual campsites as widely separated as possible to give the illusion of solitude.

Europeans bring a different set of expectations to the experience. They see camping as an economical form of travel and a good way to meet people. The campgrounds are often scenic places, located in countrylike settings with trees, grass, a river, a lake or even an ocean—but they may be within a short bus or subway ride of a large city, or even within the city itself. Wilderness they're not. Others in rural or resort areas may be self-contained vacation communities where people leave tents or trailers that become their summer homes.

But nobody is playing pioneer. Instead of sitting around a bonfire in the evening Europeans go to the camp bar or cafe or disco and socialize. And European campgrounds are almost never "full." They'll accept as many people as can find a place to squeeze in, and it's usually first come, first serve—no reservations. Once we got over our American territorial sensitivities we found that the act of squeezing in is an excellent way to meet the neighbors. The ensuing cultural exchange makes for a much richer travel experience than just pulling in to Campsite 124.

CAMPGROUND STYLE

Another feature of campgrounds is that they are safe places. When you're out adventuring on the high seas of a foreign country it's nice to pull in to a safe harbor for the night. Here you can pop your van's top, unfurl the awning, set out the folding chairs, spread out, relax, and let the kids run free and meet kids from other countries. It's always a friendly place, and there's always somebody to talk to who's been where you're headed. Everybody has the same thing in common and the same problems and everybody is there to relax and have fun.

Somebody's always offering you Italian coffee or German beer or some Greek delicacy and inviting you to sit down and chat even if you don't have a language in common. We did our bit for international relations one day in a German campground when we gave a cassette of Johnny Cash country hymns to a very grateful Hungarian country music fan. He invited us to stop in

Budapest to eat goulash with him. You can accumulate an address book full of lasting international friendships in campgrounds.

FINDING A CAMPGROUND

In the countryside you will often see signs pointing the way to campgrounds—the international logo is a silhouette of a tent and a trailer. All you have to do is follow the arrows to your haven for the night. But finding a camping place in a large city can be stressful, especially if you arrive at rush hour. Before you approach a town or tourist destination of any size, try to arm yourself with at least a rudimentary map of the area, preferably one that shows the general location of campgrounds. Failing that, take a deep breath, proceed into town and try to keep your head as you look for the tourist information office, most often signposted as "i" (for information), or campground direction signs. If you have to fall back on asking directions from passersby (or cab drivers) the word "camping" is universally understood to mean "campground." Arriving at a new city on Sunday is an alternate strategy. The traffic will be nonexistent, but of course the tourist office will be closed so you will have to depend on finding campground signs.

Campground reservations are never necessary nor even possible in most cases, but for those who like to plan ahead, the best (but by no means complete) directory is *AA Camping and Caravanning in Europe,* which is published by the Automobile Association of Great Britain. It is not widely available in North America, but can be ordered from the Automobile Association at Fanum House, Basingstoke, Hants., RG21 2EA. It includes neither Turkey nor the British Isles. Another listing, and one that your motorhome rental agency will probably supply, is *Europa Camping,* which also leaves out some good places, but does cover Great Britain and Turkey. In North America you can buy it at many travel bookstores, or from Recreational Equipment Incorporated (REI) stores. Both guides give only sketchy directions to campground locations.

CAMPGROUND PROCEDURE

When you enter the grounds, you will find before you an office marked "Reception" (or some linguistic variant thereof). Park before you proceed any further and go in and register. Rates are usually posted in several languages and are based on the size of your vehicle, the number of people, and whether you will be using hook-ups.

Prices vary wildly from country to country, and even from campground to campground, and they are not necessarily related to the luxuriousness of the facilities. The cheapest we have ever paid was in Portugal several years ago—$2.10 a night for a beautiful place that sported a gigantic swimming pool, tennis courts, several cafes, and a supermarket. At the same time we heard rumors of $25 camps elsewhere that were piled high with drifts of litter. But the average for two people in a van or motorhome without hookups is $10 to $12. As a general rule of thumb, campgrounds not listed in directories are cheaper. You are expected to pay when you leave, and more and more campgrounds are accepting Visa cards. You will usually be directed to a bank if you try to pay with a traveler's check.

When you register, the reception clerk will ask to see your passport, as they are required to do by law. Then, to keep you from skipping out on the bill, they will want to hang onto it. This is when you need an *International Camping Carnet,* which is accepted as hostage instead of your passport at campgrounds almost everywhere. (See chapter I for the details on how to get it.) The International Driver's License also works here sometimes.

CONVENIENCES TO EXPECT IN A CAMPGROUND

Every campground will, of course, have one or more buildings with toilets, wash basins, and showers. Usually there is hot water during at least part of the day, but sometimes you have to pay for it with a token you get from the reception office and then insert into a meter in the shower when you're ready to soap up. There will also be a dishwashing and food preparation area, and a different area for clothes-washing. Occasionally there will be a laundromat, but don't count on it.

In your campsite (or "pitch") there will be no firepit because open fires are *never* allowed. Nor will you be provided with a picnic table. If you want to eat outside you might invest in a light folding table and chairs. (Some people swear by this equipment, but we always find that storing it crowds our interior space too much when we're freecamping or it's raining.) There will almost always be a nice little restaurant/bar and a camp store, and sometimes a playground, a swimming pool, a tennis court, an ice cream stand, even a gift shop or a disco.

CAMPGROUND HOURS AND OTHER CUSTOMS

For quiet and security, the gates of campgrounds are often locked to cars at 10 p.m. or thereabouts, so do not plan on driving on the highway until late or taking your vehicle out, once you've arrived, for a night on the town, unless you make special arrangements with the staff.

You can, however, take a bus or taxi or subway into town and walk back through the gates after hours when you return. It's better not to park your rig in the city at night anyway. If you vacate your campsite during the day, you can hold your place by putting down the red triangle with which your vehicle should be equipped.

Beware of lunch hour closing. Like everybody else in Europe, campground workers shut the office and go home to eat from twelve to two. Often they also lock the car gate. If you're planning to check out at that time, or even to drive out for an afternoon's sightseeing, you're out of luck until they come back.

People are friendly in campgrounds, but also careful not to intrude on one another's privacy. Chatting with other campers is a pleasant way to find out about road conditions and worthwhile sights on tomorrow's journey. You will, of course, keep your radio and voices low (we Americans tend to talk more loudly than some other nationalities, we notice), and it goes without saying that you'll take care to dump your waste water and litter in the proper place.

DUMPSTATIONS AND RECYCLING

Holding tanks are a fairly new idea in Europe and so you may have to search a bit to find a campground with a dumpstation. The German automobile club ADAC publishes a helpful list and map, available at their offices free to most auto club members, of all the dump-stations in Europe. The word is "Entsorgungskanal" in German, "scarigare" in Italian, and "vidoir" in French. It is, rightly, considered an unthinkable act to dump your tanks by the highway or in a field, and may earn you a hefty fine or even a prison sentence. So don't even think about it, no matter if you're overflowing. Also be aware that it is an expected courtesy to return your vehicle to the rental agency with empty tanks. Sometimes a campground director will allow you to come in and dump for a small fee without staying overnight.

Europeans have recycled glass for many years, so don't toss that wine bottle in the garbage. Most campgrounds, some reststops, and even city streets will have separate containers for brown, green, or white glass, and also bins for clean paper. Inexplicably, aluminum is very seldom separated from the trash.

LAUNDRY

Keeping enough clean clothes on hand takes a little attention now and again. Laundromats are difficult to find in some European countries, and when you do find one it can be very expensive. (Two small loads and a partial dry cost us almost twelve dollars in Gironde, France recently.)

Consequently, most campgrounds are festooned with clotheslines strung between trees. Actually, it's kind of fun to rub out a few things in a basin while you enjoy the sunshine through the leaves. Dishwashing liquid does the job quite adequately, and a short piece of rope and a few clothespins are all the equipment you need.

On days when you're on the road or it's raining a lot, it helps to keep ahead of the game if you rinse out a pair of socks and underwear in the morning with the hot water left over from the coffee, and hang them up on a hook somewhere inside the motorhome to dry while you're rolling on. But you'll probably want to save up the jeans and towels for that once-in-a-blue-moon laundromat.

SOME BARE FACTS

A delightful alternative—and one that saves on laundry—is to stay at one of Europe's many clothing-optional campgrounds. These are usually designated by the initials FKK (Frei Körper Kultur), the name of the German naturist movement. They range from deluxe resorts to primitive camps at remote unspoiled beaches and lakes. These camps require no official memberships. You do usually need an official FKK Guidebook to find them, however. Send for the English language editon of FKK Urlaubsführer Europa, Geobuch-Verlag, Schleissheimer Strasse 371b, 8000 München 45, Germany. A second, but less authoritative source of naturist locations is the international nudist guide available from the American Sunbathing Association, 1703 N. Main Street, Kissimmee, Florida 32743. Or INF World Naturism Handbook, published in the Netherlands and distributed in the U.S. by Elysium, 700 Robinson Rd., Topanga, CA 90290.

In general, Europeans are much more comfortable with public nudity than Americans. At almost any beach, women casually shed their tops to enjoy the sun and people change clothes freely without huddling under a towel. A clothing-optional section of a beach is sometimes indicated simply by the letters "FKK" painted on a boulder. You may think that you are too modest to go public in the buff, but we guarantee that after one hour of sun and sea on your bare skin (with nobody leering, because it's not unusual), you'll never want to go back to that soggy bathing suit.

Just be sure to put sunscreen on places where the sun has never shone before, to avoid the dread new-nudist condition known affectionately as "rosy bottom."

THREE CAMPGROUNDS YOU'LL PROBABLY ENCOUNTER

Any extended circuit of Europe will certainly include London and Paris, and probably Munich, and so—just to give you a feel for the thing—here is a discussion of the campground ambience and options in those cities.

London

Inexplicably, this gigantic metropolis with its thousands of tourists offers only one choice for people in vans and motorhomes who want to stay in the city: the Crystal Palace Caravan Harbour in Bromley. Happily, that choice is a good one. The campground is situated at the top of a breezy hill overlooking the city, in the midst of an extensive grassy park with great old trees and a children's zoo, swimming pool, and tennis courts. It is run by the British Caravan Club for its members, but an International Camping Carnet (see Chapter I) will also get you in, *and* get you a 20% discount.

The campground lies at the base of the BBC radio transmitter. Red double-decker city buses stop outside the gates (#11 takes the same route as the tour buses) and it is a short walk to the BritRail Station. There are shops, laundromats, restaurants and take-outs nearby, in a neighborhood which is not posh but pleasant enough. Crystal Palace is a very soothing place to return to after a hectic day in the noisy city, although in midsummer it does get pretty crowded.

But this is more than just a pleasant city campground. The area is full of history and mystery. The camp itself is built on the exact spot where once stood the Crystal Palace, a magnificent iron and glass structure constructed for the Great Exhibition of 1851, the first international trade fair. For a time it was one of the wonders of the world, and then in 1936 it mysteriously and tragically burned to the ground. In the huge park which formed its grounds you can still see stone sphynxes on ruined Gothic terraces, monster-statues looming through the bushes, and a Victorian hedge-maze.

London itself is a maze. Trying to find the Crystal Palace Caravan Harbour from the sketchy directions in the *Europa* guide took us three desperate hours the first time we tried it, plus two SOS phone calls to the camp management. Now that we've sorted it out, you should have no trouble. (Although we do recommend that you buy a copy of the map book *London A to Z*—fondly known as the "A to Zed"—as soon as you can find a parking place near a tobacconist's.)

Coming in to London from the east on the A-2, get off on the A205, which will be signposted frequently as the South Circular Road. Follow its windings through the city to Dulwich, where you will spot the Crystal Palace signs and the camping symbol.

If you don't mind a long subway or bus ride into the city, Abbey Wood campground on the far east side of London is an alternative to the inner-city feel of Crystal Palace. It is larger, more deluxe, and more expensive.

Paris

At first glance, the City of Light, too, seems to offer only one possibility for campers, but a more sophisticated approach discloses several additional options.

The obvious place to stay, and one where hundreds and hundreds of campers *do* stay, is the huge municipal campground in the Bois de Boulogne. The ambience is bustling, noisy, efficient—a small city within a city. Its main advantage is its location in the heart of Paris.

But this turns out to be a delusion. It is a twenty-minute bus ride (not counting the wait for departures) from the campground gates around through the park to the metro, and this is the only way to connect with the public transportation in the city. By contrast, the train from the charming town of Versailles gets you into the very heart of the Paris metro system in that same twenty minutes, and the walk from the campground to the station is a short three blocks. The Camping Municipal de Porchefontaine in Versailles is a tranquil haven of cool shade under towering beech and chestnut trees on the edge of a dense forest. The management is friendly and welcoming, and although the showers are the infuriating French type where you must constantly push a button, there is usually plenty of hot water and the washrooms are heated in chilly weather. However, be warned that the toilets are squats and the showers are none too clean—a situation that is usual in France—and you may have to use your jack to get level. The camp ground is open from March 18 to October 21, and does fill up in July and August, as might be expected.

Again, we had a hard time finding it, but you won't, if you follow our directions. Start at the Chateau in Versailles (all roads and signs lead to it). Take the Avenue du Paris (the main street leading directly away from the main entrance of the Chateau), turn right at the double gatehouses onto Rue de Porchefontaine, follow the signs down Rue Coste to the end, turn left one block to Bertholet and the campground entrance.

There are several other savvy Paris options to the Bois de Boulogne. All are in more or less outlying areas: Tremblay at Champigny-Sur-Marne is twelve kilometers southeast; Paris Sud at Choisy-Le-Roi is fourteen kilometers southeast, and Airotel International at Maisons-Laffitte is sixteen kilometers west.

Munich

Although there are several other possibilities for a place from which to explore the delightful Bavarian capital, nobody with any feel for gemutlichkeit would go anyplace but Thalkirchen. This big joyous campground on the Isar River is the absolute epitome of what international motorhoming ought to be. Here you can talk business over a Weissbier with a Hungarian Adidas impresario, share Swiss chocolate and politics with a South African couple, and discuss wine with a professor of rhetoric from Italy. Later you can invite a Scottish fire-eater to dinner. We speak from experience.

Thalkirchen is situated "im grunen Wald"—in the green forest, through which runs the even greener Isar River. Campers can loll on lush lawns and watch the surfers (yes, *surfers*) mount the stationary wave under the bridge, or swim in the lake that widens out at the foot of the lawn, or wave to parties of merry-makers gliding downstream on log rafts. A convenient bus takes you into town in half an hour to explore the rich cultural and architectural treasures of Munich. Later, back at camp, the cafes and several bars are the scene of international gemutlichkeit far into the night. There's a laundromat, too.

In case you can't get in at Oktoberfest (in late *September*), when the whole world comes to Munich to drink beer, there are three other (pale) options for camping: Langwieder See at Eschenriederstrasse 119, Nord-West at Dachauerstrasse 571, and Munchen-Obermenzing, at Lochhausener Strasse 59 in Obermenzing.

COUNTRY-BY-COUNTRY TIPS

Netherlands - Although directories still list it, the campground at the Olympic Stadium in Amsterdam no longer exists. An out-of-town alternative is Gaasper Camping (take the highway south toward Utrecht and get off at Gaasperdamweg). There is a subway stop just 100 meters from the camp.

England - If you're going to be spending several weeks in England and Scotland, you may want to join the British Caravan Club before you go. (The Caravan Club, East Grinstead House, East Grinstead, West Sussex, England, RH19 1UA, about $40) Your membership, among other benefits, entitles you to a book and map listing 183 campgrounds (or "caravansites") run by the club and 4400 Certified Locations (five-van sites on farms). Also, their Foreign Towing Handbook and Directory lists much information on campgrounds on the Continent.

France - Typically enough, French campgrounds are rated on a star system in Michelin's *Camping and Caravanning in France*. In the Loire Valley region the Castel et Camping-Caravanning chain maintains campgrounds in and around ancient castles, or chateaus. The French Riviera is spectacularly inhospitable to camping vehicles in towns (although there are some good campgrounds, especially near Nice and Antibes). Motorhomes and vans that park, even for a moment, in Cannes or anyplace in the entire country of Monaco are in danger of being towed away, and many parking lots in other towns have "van guards," or horizontal bars six feet above the ground, at the entrance.

Spain - Sadly, almost the entire east and south coast of Spain has become a solid concrete Iberian Miami Beach. People who haven't been there recently will often recommend the south coast area between Almeria and Motril, but its former peaceful beauty is now disfigured by "polyethylene plantations," or greenhose farms, and consequent polluted air and water and piles of trash. Elsewhere in Spain the camping places are some of the most delightful in Europe: the grounds are luxuriant with flowering vines and cages of songbirds; there are resident dogs and cats, and the washrooms are large, clean, and lined with beautiful Spanish tile. But be careful when asking directions: "campo" means field; the word you want is "campiamento."

Portugal - Here the same caution prevails for the same reason. Ask for the "campismo." The Portuguese, who are remarkably relaxed about everything else, have a passion for paperwork, so when you pull into a campground there, be prepared to be patient while they ask you your grandmother's maiden name and fill out everything by hand in triplicate. In Lisbon the municipal campground has become a shantytown for Angolan refugees, so when you visit that city, it is better to take the forty-five-minute scenic drive south to the fishing village of Sesimbra. There you will find a municipal campground high on the cliffs within the massive ramparts of a ruined Moorish fort, where you can enjoy spectacular views of the harbor below with its red and yellow fishing boats.

Greece - The beaches, villages, and ancient ruins of Hellas are the sites for some of the loveliest camping in the world. Campgrounds run by the government (marked "EOT") are especially clean and well-kept, with a sense of national pride. Unfortunately, the only campground in Athens is a spectacular exception to the general excellence; it is crowded, noisy, and inconveniently located in a smoggy industrial district where there is no place to buy a meal or even groceries. Strangely enough, almost nobody takes motorhomes to the Greek islands, although we have found this to be perfectly possible if you are willing to freecamp.

Eastern Europe - As the spirit of capitalism revives in eastern Europe, some countries which were formerly part of the Soviet Bloc are now geared up for tourism; others not. Travelers are rediscovering the beauties of the Czech countryside and the delights of Prague. Excellent small campgrounds abound, many of them among the roses and cabbage patches of former private back gardens. In Prague, the owners of the large older houses on Trojska Street in the wooded suburb of Troja have added modern camping facilities and charming cafes to their backyard apple orchards. Eastern Germany and Hungary, too, have some pleasant campgrounds and good tourist facilities, but Poland, Romania, and Bulgaria are still struggling Third World economies and not yet ready for vacationers.

GREAT CAMPGROUNDS - A PERSONAL SAMPLER

Armenistis Beach, Chalkidiki Peninsula, Greece - Simple facilities amid pines and heather and golden sands, a windsurfing school and an open-air dining pavilion where the food is Greek and the bouzouki music and dancing are spontaneous, and you will be the only Americans.

Sindicato Dos Bancarios Do Sul E Ilhas, Olhao, Portugal - Giant swimming pool, supermarket, lawns and pines surrounding a ruined mansion, near a fascinating and unspoiled fishing village and islands and a nature reserve. Very cheap.

Les Sables d'Or, Cap Ferrat, near Bordeaux, France - Civilized French comfort on a skinny peninsula like Cape Cod. Wild Atlantic dunes and a ferny forest with trails and picnic glades nearby.

Mala Duba, Dalmatian coast south of Makarska, Croatia - A hidden cove thick with pine and fig trees, a pebbly beach, warm dark blue sea, a tiny outdoor cafe— and *no clothes.*

Fusina, across the lagoon from Venice, Italy - Mosquitoes, a thumping disco, but next to a dock where you can catch a motor launch for a breathtaking first approach to Venice by sea.

Önder Camping, Kusadasi, Turkey - Hospitable, clean, cheap, nice trees and flowers, an excellent restaurant, and within walking distance of the action in this best of all Turkish tourist shopping towns.

Zugligeti Niche, Budapest, Hungary - A lovely wooded ravine in the Buda Hills with a friendly English-speaking staff and a charming restaurant. Next to the chair-lift which soars up the mountain to the Elizabeth Tower, where you can enjoy a breathtaking view of the city and surrounding countryside.

FREECAMPING

Spontaneity is one of the best reasons for choosing to travel by van or motorhome in the first place. You want to be able to go when you please and stop when you feel like it. A campground doesn't always need to be your destination at the end of the day. In Europe it is perfectly possible to freecamp, if you use a little know-how.

"But isn't that dangerous?" people often ask us. "Don't the police bother you?" In America both these worries are realistic. But in Europe things are much more relaxed. Nobody minds if you play it by ear about where you spend the night, providing the place is appropriate and you are not noisy and don't leave litter. True, a few countries do have laws about where you are allowed to camp, but they are seldom enforced.

When we are on the road we stay at campgrounds only once every three or four nights. One year we freecamped for the whole three months of our trip, and we kept perfectly happy, healthy, and clean. For the answer to the obvious question, see the next chapter.

"YOU CAMPED WHERE?"

In the interests of spontaneity we have stayed in some outrageous freecamping spots just to say we did. In Paris we have lived in our van at the foot of the Eiffel Tower and beside the lake in the Bois de Vincennes. We have parked happily overnight on the quay by the Seine and even in the most elegant square in Paris, the Place du Vosges. In London we spent ten lovely days sleeping beside the roses in Regent's Park, then moved to a mews behind a friend's house in the district called Swiss Cottage, and later stayed beside the canals in the heart of the city. In Munich we slept behind the Deutsches Museum until the stares of the stone monsters bothered us, then we shifted to the street edging the Englischer Garten in Schwabing. Once we lasted a week in the lakeside parking lot of the most elegant hotel in Montreux before a traffic cop nicely asked us to be gone before tomorrow night.

And so on. We used to be crazier when we were younger. Now that we're older and know more, we realize that although most of these places were fun, they were probably not very safe nor very legal. We are too wise and too chicken to stay in such places now, and we wouldn't recommend that you do, either. Nowadays, we strongly suggest that in cities you go to a campground. But if you really must wing it, try the streets bordering parks, but not in the park. Or seek out parking lots of stadiums or hospitals or supermarkets, if they're not too lonely, and park in a spot under a light. Avoid residential areas unless you're visiting a resident (you'll worry the homeowners) and factory districts (lonely at night, noisy in the morning, and often smelly).

CHOOSING A RURAL FREECAMP

In the countryside finding a sleepsite is much more relaxed and pleasant. Really, there are only four essential questions to ask when you're evaluating a spot:

1. *Is it level?* Or can you get it level by using your jack or by driving one wheel up on a rock or board? Otherwise you may find all the food slopping over to one side of the pan when you try to cook, and all of you slopping over to one side of the bed when you try to sleep. This problem sometimes presents itself not only in the wilds, but in curbside town parking because of the slope of the street.

2. *Is it safe?* Remote or isolated areas are usually okay if you're near a moderately well-traveled road, but if you see shards of broken auto glass on the ground or signs warning of theft, travel on. The most reassuring situation is to find one or two other campers in a place where you're planning to sleep. But be aware that a large gathering of trailers and motorhomes in a field,

without a campground sign, is more than likely to be a gypsy camp, where you will be welcome only as prey.

3. *Is it quiet enough for sleep?* This varies with your own tolerance for noise and the degree of soundproofing of your vehicle. In general, you want to get a bit away from the edge of the highway—although personally we find the nocturnal sound of whooshing trucks a nostalgic white noise. Late-night restaurants and bars and gas stations can also be disturbing. But the most disturbing sound of all is the whine of even a single mosquito. Carry repellent and don't park by boggy lakes or slow-moving streams or trash dumps.

4. *Is somebody going to wake you up and ask you to move?* Like the police, perhaps? Although this is highly unlikely, it can happen if you've not bothered to look up signs in your phrase book that you don't understand. We, for example, got roused up by a fire warden once in Germany because we were blocking a well-posted fire lane. (See the chapter on "Roads and Driving" for a list of "No Parking" signs) Or, if you've chosen a large empty lot next to an office building, an irate worker may want you to give him his parking place early next morning. Or if you've pulled off into a construction site, the builder may come along at dawn with his bulldozer. The moral is— think ahead.

Usually it is so easy to spot places that pass this four-question test that you can go on for a few miles until you find a sleepsite that is just perfect and has:

5. *Toilets* Convenient, but not essential. Read the next chapter to find out why.

6. *A Beautiful Setting* A flowery meadow, a mysterious ivy-draped forest, a cliff overlooking the ocean, a rocky lakeshore... The possiblities are endlessly varied.

7. *A Beautiful View* Rolling green hills, the vast ocean, fearsome chasms, distant winding river valleys... Again, a cornucopia of wonders.

8. *Beautiful Sounds* Crickets, surf, a brook, nightingales, church bells... Pleasant dreams!

What to Look For

Now let's go back and get specific. Here you are at five o'clock, tired, beginning to be hungry, barreling down the road looking for your haven of rest. Exactly what kinds of places should you look for as you whiz by? (And start looking *now*. Few things are more frustrating than trying to find a freecamp in the dark.)

If you are traveling on the autobahn, the autoroute, the autopista, or other national highway, look for a big blue and white "P" sign and pull off into a rest stop for the night. These are always our first choice. They are convenient, free, safe, and relatively quiet, and usually beautifully planted to take advantage of the natural landscape. You are not only allowed, but expected to spend the night. There are usually—but not always—toilets and washbasins.

Rest stops are especially good in France and Germany, where we often get on the highway just to find one for the night. Even if we have to pay a small toll in France and Italy, it's worth it. In England, theoretically there is a £3.50 charge for a stay over two hours, but this is seldom actually enforced. For maximum quiet, be sure to notice where the truck lanes are

Sleeping in the Best Places

The "P" sign, this one heralding a rest area with picnic facilities 12 km further on, and reminding you of the one coming up in 300 meters. (Photo by David Shore)

and settle yourself as far away from their noise as possible. You can often park quite a way back in the forest, and once we even found an aire with its own little lake.

In Spain and Portugal, where the national roads are as good as the toll motorways (and more scenic), your first impulse should be to look for a restaurant, or *hostal,* with a large parking lot. Overnighting is okay in such places, but it is usually a good idea to go in and have at least a cup of coffee so the owners know that you are potential customers. Park far away from the doors so the departing midnight guests won't wake you up. An abandoned hostal is, of course, even better for your purposes.

Off the major highways, in forested country, side roads can yield wonderful spots in clearings and glades, or a large lay-by on a quiet lane. In grassy or flat wild areas, watch for a line of trees in the distance that could mark a creek, or find a lake on your map. The banks of these bodies of water can be lovely camping spots. Watch also for abandoned quarries, although these are not as pleasant.

When you are driving through more built-up areas, look for yacht harbors and marinas (where people are used to seeing vehicles parked overnight), or tuck yourself into an obscure corner of a large parking lot. One couple we know stays almost every night in the vast lots of hypermarches (supermarkets). We prefer the parking areas belonging to tourist attractions like ancient ruins, caves, natural wonders, castles, etc. The guard is used to seeing motorhomes there, and if he or anybody else questions you, you can always say you're waiting to get in the morning. Such spots have the great advantage of giving you a crack at the wonder early in the day before the tourist buses arrive. Of course, if "No overnight camping" signs are posted, they should be heeded.

And One That's Not So Easy

Surprisingly enough, the most difficult area for freecamping is agricultural land, especially if the region is very fertile and every little piece of dirt has been claimed by somebody for growing crops. Adding to the problem is the fact that in such territories there probably won't be any campgrounds nearby either. The main road will have no wide places in it, and small side roads usually turn out to be private driveways leading straight into a farmer's front yard, where you must maneuver a turnaround amidst barking dogs, squawking chickens, and gawking children. At this point you could probably ask the farmer or his wife if you could camp on their land, but at this point we're always too embarrassed. If you don't ask, farmers do not take kindly to your blocking their tractor roads or driving into the fields and squashing their crops.

This is a situation calling for an imaginative solution. On weekdays anyway, look for the soccer field in the nearest little town (the sign will say something like "stadion") and park in the far corner of the public lot. You'll have to wait until the locals finish their evening game, however, or you'll draw a crowd when you cook dinner. But who knows, it could turn into an adventure—as freecamping often does.

GREAT FREECAMPING SPOTS - A PERSONAL SAMPLER

Domain Estoril, Le Corniche d'Or, east of St. Raphael, Cote d'Azur, France - Maroon bluffs above azure waves in a national forest, just a few miles from the crowded snob scene of Cannes and St. Tropez.

Samos, Greece - A pine-needle-strewn glade off a steep mountain road in the island's interior, where the ancient bell of the monastery below clanged the hours.

Carrapateria, west coast of the Algarve between Sagres and Alfambra, Portugal - The ultimate freecamping beach. Acres of wild dunes and cliffs, an endless strand with waves, a warm shallow lagoon. Small town with good cafes just out of sight but feels like the end of the world.

Near Pfronten-Meilingen, Bavarian Alps, Germany - An abandoned mountainside hotel with a parking lot overlooking distant green hills, half a mile away from the tourist throngs in the village. Utterly silent except for cowbells.

Vanern, Sweden - A vast sepia lake with forested shores for camping just off the highway. Water lilies and wild raspberries.

Steinfeld in Drautal, Austria - A sandy bank under the bridge on the icy turquoise Drau River. Pebbly shores, shallow places for wading and cooling beer. Just down the railroad tracks is a cute little station where the train never stops and the toilets are never locked. Magnificent mountains and hiking.

Chapter 5

"Where do you... Uh...?"

This question is what causes travelers to waste gobs of money on uncomfortable accomodations. For the sake of a bathroom down the hall (only deluxe hotel rooms in Europe have their own baths) most tourists put up with drafty, noisy rooms, beds that cause nightmares, heaters that don't work, chambermaids who barge in, and check-out times. The wretched excess of a toilet within sleep-walking distance costs extra.

Of course, if you're driving a self-contained motorhome, you asked that question only once, when you bought or rented it. Chemical toilets are usually an option most dealers offer even for small vans, if you want to put up with the crowding and the smell. But even if you are so equipped, you won't always be near your own facilities. So read on; you'll find many of the tips in this chapter useful, and you may enjoy reading about simpler answers.

CAMPGROUNDS

Campgrounds, of course, nearly always offer clean, modern facilities. Walking to them at night is no different from walking to a hotel restoom, except that you can see the stars on the way. But there's an even more comfortable answer.

THE PO

Brace yourself now. We're going to tell you the secret

that will liberate you once and for all from plumbing dependency. It will free you to spend the night anyplace you please, with never a 3 AM worry. You may be shocked at first, but when you think about it, you'll realize it makes sense.

The solution is the po, that device that for centuries has been considered the civilized way to spare oneself that cold, jarring journey down some strange hotel hallway. A po can be any container of suitable size and shape for easy use in the middle of the night. It should be easy to rinse and keep clean, and small enough for discreet storage in the daytime. It should have a lid in case of delayed disposal.

We have found that a one-half liter yogurt container fills these qualifications quite well. It is sturdy; it rinses odor-free and clean; it's decorated with pretty flowers and can be stored in any number of nooks and crannies in the rig. And it's disposable and available all over Europe.

Privacy, or at least psychological privacy, is easily obtained, especially if your vanmate is asleep. We know some non-squeamish people who admit to emptying the po carefully down the sink drain through a small funnel and chasing it with fresh water. Decency decrees, of course, that you would never do this in a campground, and when freecamping in a public parking lot or even in the wilds you would be careful to put a bucket under the drain before you went to bed.

OTHER RESOURCES

In the daytime, of course, there are numerous opportunities to find public facilities. Large highway gas stations are well-equipped—although small ones in the country may not be. Restaurants and hotels, of course, have nice restrooms, but you usually have to be well dressed and confident enough to pass as a customer. Owners of cafes can be unpleasant if you just come in to use the facilities without at least buying a coffee or a beer. Parks in Europe, unlike those in North America, usually have few or no public bathrooms. Coin-operated kiosks are a high-tech option that is often seen in France, as are outdoor pissoirs. Anybody foolhardy enough to use the restrooms in a subway or a public square in a city will probably have an unpleasant experience that will make a colorful story later. It is far preferable to seek out a department store, museum, or cathedral. And never leave a tourist attraction, theater or (most especially) a beer drinking place without taking advantage of the facilities.

But Sundays, unexpected holidays and early closing times will sometimes find you pounding on closed doors. In that case, walk the necessary several blocks to the railway station, where the restrooms will not be free, but at least they'll be open twenty-four hours a day. Or go back to your own home on wheels, draw the curtains and use the po.

HOW TO ASK

Many people find it embarrassing to ask to use the facilities, and no one likes to make a scene by fumbling around between languages with this request. Even when the language is English, it is hard for North Americans to say the plain word "toilet," which is the commonly used term in Great Britain. The Americanism "restroom" will get you funny looks, or perhaps a room with a bed.

The following list will help you ask politely and descreetly:

English: Where is the lavatory, please? (or the WC)

French: Ou sont les toilettes, s'il vous plait? (Oo sohn lay twa-*lett*, see-voo-play?)

German: Wo sind die toiletten, bitte? (Vo zind dee toy-*let*-ten, bitteh?)

Greek: Too-ah-*let*-Ah?

Italian: Dove ce il gambinetto, per favore? (Do-vay say el gahm-bee-*nay*-to, pear fah-*vo*-ray?)

Spanish: Donde estan los servicios, por favor? (Doan-day estahn los ser-*vee*-thee-os, por fah-*vor*?)

THE DREADED SQUAT

In Southern Europe, including France, you will undoubtedly encounter facilities virtually unknown to North Americans. David tells of his first encounter with what we later came to call a "squat."

"There was a urinal on one wall, and a door. Since I was looking for more than a urinal, I stepped through the door, expecting to find a commode. What greeted me looked like a shower stall. But there was no shower. Only a porcelain floor with a drain hole in the middle and two treads on which to place one's feet. At first I recoiled in horror, but since it was the only game in town, I decided to try it. I didn't like it. To add to my horror, it flushed automatically and unexpectedly. The water swirled furiously around my feet. I felt like I was squatting on two rocks in the Colorado River. Small rocks."

In defense of the squat, it should be said that it is more hygienic than the standard arrangement because only the soles of your feet touch anything, and doctors claim that the necessary position, while precarious in high heels, is better for proper function. The automatic flush that David experienced is the exception rather than the rule. Two tips: face the door before assuming the attitude, and afterward unlock the door and get ready to jump out of the way before you flush.

THE DRAGON

Another aspect of European public plumbing that can be disturbing at first is the almost ubiquitous presence of a person we have come to call The Dragon. Like Fafner curled around his magic horde, the Dragon guards the entrance to the john. Sitting at a little table, she demands a piece of silver before you can enter. Payment is usually the second smallest coin of the national currency. There will be a sign on a little plate, or she'll tell you plainly in a loud, annoyed voice. Dragons are always angry. But wouldn't you be if you had to spend your life in such a working environment?

The money is not a tip, as many tourists assume, nor is it voluntary. You *must* pay her, or she'll make a scene. Those coins on the table are wages for the Dragon, and she works hard for them, keeping the premises clean and functioning.

BATHING

European campgrounds nearly always have hot showers, unlike many North American motorcamps. There are a few regional peculiarities, however. In many parts of Europe you may have to pay the camp office for a token which you drop in a meter box for exactly four minutes of hot water. In France you must push a button every ten seconds or so to keep the water flowing—experienced campers learn to lean on it with elbow or back, without even cursing very much. A lightweight cosmetic or shaving case is handy, especially if it has a loop for hanging it up in the shower booth. Plastic or rubber sandals are also a good idea.

If you're freecamping in a van without a shower, you'll need to improvise to keep clean. Sponge baths are basic in-van hygiene. Showers and baths are not hard to find if you know where to look. In most European cities there are public showers in the railroad stations, and sometimes in other locations around town. Prices vary, but they average around three dollars or less. Showers at large highway rest stops are beginning to be provided, especially in Germany, Switzerland, Austria, and Belgium. At rest stops in France men can sometimes bluff their way into the public showers for truckers by tipping the attendant and demanding the key ("Le clef!") Some campgrounds will let you take a shower for a small charge without checking in.

Cold showers are also available on most Southern European beaches, epecially in France. We came to prefer them in warm summer weather. Or you can simply take a lovely swim (soapless, please) in a handy lake or river in the country (but remember that bodies of water in cities may be polluted). Or, failing all else, you can pay to go into a municipal swimming pool and use their showers.

A BATH IN A BASIN

In a pinch, a bath in an inch of water is not only quite possible but quite refreshing. A flat-bottomed receptacle big enough for your feet is best. A dishpan works all right, but the really ideal bath-basin is a wide, flat motor-oil draining pan, which you can get at auto supply shops for less than a dollar. Send your partner for a walk, draw the van curtains, boil up a pot of water, and pour it in the basin. Then add cool water until it's the right temperature. Wash your face first, with clear water, and then dry it. Now put the basin on the floor, step into it, rub a little soap on a wash cloth and proceed. Rinse and dry each section as you go, to keep from getting chilled. Afterward you'll feel quite pleased with yourself.

Chapter 6

Language:
Easier Than You Think

"But how do you manage when you can't speak the language?" This is a question we are often asked. It's true that motorhoming brings you much closer to local people than hotel-and-restaurant travel, and sometimes you need and want to talk with these folks. This is not the major difficulty that first-time motorhomers imagine. We speak just a little bit of German and Spanish, and we get along just fine. So can you.

In Western Europe, English is fast becoming the universal language, the lingua franca of commerce and travel. We keep a list of "international" English words, and add to it all the time. Recently, for example, we were interested to see that "ticket" had replaced "billet" on the signs on the French autoroute. Other such widely understood words are "stop," "parking," "supermarket," "problem," "color film," "telephone," "baby," "radio," "auto," "cigarette," "jeans, "jazz," "rock," "television," and on and on. Most young people have studied English in school, and in Northern Europe almost everyone under the age of fifty speaks it fluently.

Inevitably you will occasionally find yourself in situations where out of necessity or courtesy you need to communicate with someone who speaks no English. At this point many of us panic, as if we were trying to talk to Martians. Relax, keep your sense of humor, and bear in mind that you are facing another human being who wants to communicate with *you* and is used to the idea that people often speak different languages. A smile helps a lot, and it is surprising what you can get across with gestures. Remember not to raise your voice; it only makes people upset.

ROAD SIGNS

But what about road signs? Will you be able to read directions and safety warnings? Highway engineers on the Continent are just as eager as you are that drivers should be able to understand signs quickly and easily, and so most countries make wide use of the international symbols and stick figures that you will find illustrated in the "Roads and Driving" chapter. Off the highway, however, you may need to refer occasionally to your phrase book to interpret street signs.

And we do recommend that you take phrase books for most of the languages you will be encountering. Buy them before you leave; they can be hard to find once you're abroad. The most widely available are the Berlitz guides, which are easy to use, although they are based on British English and include ridiculous phrases like "Where can I get this suit invisibly mended?" Preferable, if you can find them, are the "Just Enough" series of Passport Books.

But don't be intimidated by the idea that you have to memorize all those pages and pages of strange sentences. You don't. Language guidebooks take it as their mission to teach you to speak grammatically and in elaborate complete sentences. In real life, one word, astutely applied, will do the trick. For instance, contrast:

1. "May I ask, if you would be so kind, sir, as to direct me to the men's toilets?"

2. "Toilets?" (asked courteously, with a smile)

The second will get you there just as well, and probably faster.

TWENTY-ONE MAGIC WORDS

Over the years we have evolved a very short minimum list of words that will get you through most daily situations quite comfortably. These magic twenty-one are, in order of importance:

- Please
- Thank you
- Hello
- Goodbye
- Yes
- No
- Good
- Toilets
- How much?
- One
- Two
- Half
- Excuse me
- Where is...?
- Do you have...?
- Beautiful
- Water
- Bread
- Milk
- Beer
- Wine

For most Western European languages you will find that you already know several of these, and that several more are similar to English. Look up the magic twenty-one in your phrase book the night before you cross the border (imminent need is a powerful learning incentive), memorize them, practice out loud a bit, and you'll be all set to go shopping, order food in a restaurant, ask directions, buy fuel, and make friends, even if nobody around speaks a word of English. With this foundation, you'll be surprised how quickly you'll pick up other words from signs and billboards without even trying. But always remember that a smile and a friendly manner are the most important items in your vocabulary.

COUNTRY-BY-COUNTRY TIPS

Great Britain

It's the same language, but sometimes you may wonder, especially when buying food. Zucchini squash is "vegetable marrow" if large, and "courgettes" if small. Stringbeans are "haricots," and eggplant is "aubergine." "Crisps" are what we call chips, and "chips" are what we call French fries. The names of auto parts, too, can be surprising: "bonnet" for the hood, "hood" for the top, and "boot" for the trunk. European English is British English for the most part, so these variations prevail all over the Continent. "Petrol," for gasoline, is an important example.

Netherlands

Here's one country where you won't need to arm yourself with a phrase book, because nearly everyone speaks English. It is, however, a friendly gesture to learn a few courtesy words in Dutch, such as:

- *Alstublieft (ahls too bleeft)* - Please
- *Bedankt (beh-dahnkt)* - Thank you
- *Dag! (dahk!)* - Hello or goodbye

Scandinavia

Here are another three countries (Denmark, Norway, and Sweden) where you won't need a phrase book. Nearly everyone speaks English here.

France

Ah, but the citizens of la belle France have strong opinions about their language. They feel that dogs bark, cats meow, and human beings speak French. Any other kinds of words you speak to them they regard as mere uncouth noise.

However, we have discovered that any earnest attempt at French, no matter how clumsy, will soften Gallic hearts. Our favorite sentence, and one we use often, is "Pardon ma gaucherie; je ne comprend pas Francais." (Excuse my stupidity; I don't speak French.") This at least shows a willingness to try, and often causes the listener to speak English rather than hear French spoken so badly.

Germany

Shopkeepers here usually have quite a bit of English, and most people have studied it in school and speak quite well. But it's courteous to learn a few German phrases anyway, like:

- *Guten tag (gooten tahg)* - good day (north Germany)
- *Grüss Gott (groos goht)* - hello (literally "God's greeting" - used in Bavaria and Austria)
- *Bitte (bitteh)* - please
- *Danke (donkeh)* - thank you
- *Wiedersehn!* (veeder sayn) - Goodbye. What you say when you leave a shop.

However, if you're going to do any boning up on languages before your trip, we recommend that you give German top priority because it is the language of tourism in Europe.

Greece

An impossibly difficult language for the casual traveler, but the Greeks are lovely people and will help. Many Greek men have spent their youth working in the U.S. and speak excellent American English. The Cyrillic alphabet can be confusing (learn the capital letters, at least, so you can read street signs) and the gesture language is different. A Greek nods his head up and down for "no" (and says "oh yeh") and shakes it for "yes" (and says "nay"). Even some Greeks who speak English do this, and it can be a real booby trap if you aren't constantly aware. A phrase book will help here.

Italy

The Italians are as monolingual as the French, but they are much nicer about it. Gestures go a long way here, but you'll need a phrase book to really communicate.

Portugal

The people here are kind and helpful and appreciative of any fumbling attempts on your part to wrap your tongue around their difficult words. We have found that most Portuguese can understand (but not speak) Spanish if you talk slowly and clearly. Because of the pronunciation problems, a phrase book doesn't help much, but you can get by as long as you know that "retretes" (ray-*tray*-tays) means bathrooms.

Language

Spain

Courtesy is extremely important to the proud Spaniards, and to be abrupt and efficient is considered rude. Attempt pleasantries, even if it's only a nod and a smile. Only in central Spain will the spoken word correspond exactly with your phrase book. Regional dialects, such as Andalusian, can be very different, and Catalan, in the northeast, and Euskadi, in the Basque country, are entirely separate languages. Almost everyone, however, understands Castilian, or standard Spanish, even if they don't speak it.

Turkey

A phrase book is absolutely essential here, because few Turkish words are like any other words you know. But the Turks don't expect you to attempt their language and will take all the responsibility for communication themselves. German is the tourist lingua franca, because many Turks are "guest workers" for part of the year in that country.

Czech Republic and Hungary

You can be excused for not learning all twenty-one of the magic words in these tongue-twisting consonant-filled languages. Work on your German instead; most people you meet will have at least a smattering of that language and will expect to communicate with tourists in it.

CROSSED WIRES

Familiar Words That Mean Something Else In Europe

Menu: The prix fixe meal, or daily special. If you want the list of dishes available, ask for "la carte."

Gas: Propane for camping stoves. The liquid that fuels your vehicle is "petrol."

Eis (pronounced "ice"): Ice cream. Frozen water in cubes is called "glace" (pronounced "glahs").

Bar: A pleasant counter for coffee or beer or wine with light food, not a dark place for getting drunk.

Caravan: A trailer, not a procession.

Particular: Private, when seen on a sign in Spain

Puxe (pronounced "push"): Pull, when seen on a door in Portugal.

REFRESHMENT SAVVY

There will inevitably come a time, perhaps every day, when after miles of sightseeing or driving you're going to want to stop for a quick one. Those of you who do soft drinks have no problem: just point. But if coffee or beer or wine is your objective, the customs are more complex, and it's fun to learn the options and the local slang.

If you want to sit, rather than drink standing up at the counter, you're going to have to pay extra for the privilege. Once in a while it's worth the price, especially if your feet are killing you. But never sit in a large choice spot that everyone else is carefully avoiding. The best known example is the empty outdoor cafe on the

Piazza San Marco in Venice, where the music of a light-classical orchestra entices unwary tourists into sitting down to be served a $15 beer.

Generally, Southern European coffee is a small cup of espresso. Refills are not part of the deal. Sugar is offered, but if you want milk or cream you have to say so at the beginning. Although the word "cafe" is universally understood to mean coffee, there are some interesting variations.

In France, "cafe au lait" is half hot milk. In Spain you can ask for "cafe con leche" for the same effect. Black coffee is "cafe noir" in France, and "cafe solo" in Spain. A "cortado" in Spain, or a cappuccino everywhere else, is not the San Francisco version with cinnamon and brandy, but espresso with a slug of steamed milk. Cappuccino is particularly superb in Italy, where you can buy it (or espresso) at the bars in highway filling stations. In Germany, ordering it "mit sahne" gets you a glop of whipped cream on top.

A short beer is simpler. In Spain ask for "una caña;" in Germany "ein pils;" in Portugal ask for a "fina." But in France, be sure to order "un demi," or run the risk of being served the most expensive bottled beer in the house. For a bigger one, say "cachi" in Spain, "cañeca" in Portugal, and for a really gigantic quaff in Germany, order a "mass."

If wine is your drink of choice, ask for a "blanco" (white), "chato" (red), or "fino" (sherry) in a Spanish bar, "weisswein" or "rotwein" in Germany, and "vin blanc" or "vin rouge" in France. But be sure to add "ordinaire" in that last-named country unless you want to pay for the best in the house.

All this colloquial correctness can go to one's head and lead to overconfidence, as David found out on our first day in Portugal. Someone had tipped him off on the hip way to order two coffees. After practicing the pronunciation, he stepped up to the bar and called out "Dos bicas!" The barman looked at him briefly and asked, "No mice?" Startled, David took a minute to collect his wits and stammer, "No thanks, just sugar." Later, of course, we found out that "nao mais" means "nothing more," which made the incident less bizarre, but more humbling.

TELEPHONES

Language can be a problem on European telephones, especially when it comes to figuring out the instructions in the phone booth for local calls. When you call home, your long-distance company may be able to provide an English-speaking operator to facilitate the connection, and sometimes (depending on the country) European operators speak English. The main post office in town will usually have a telephone room where you can throw yourself on the mercy of the clerk behind the desk. Failing that, an alternate strategy is to appeal to the campground director to set up the connection for you.

European telephones have national pecularities too complex to list here. A factor that can simplify things once you get the hang of it is that many public phones use cards rather than coins. Telephone cards are very popular and are sold by post offices, shops, and street vendors for specified amounts of phone charges. There is also a thriving collector market. If you're interested in collecting European phone cards, contact Gunther Schmidt at Hugins Telecard Service, Oliemolen 22, 1622 JK Hoorn, Holland. Tel: (31) 2290 36211. He's a knowledgeable and reputable dealer.

Chapter 7

Money
Handling It Wisely

Many travelers have questions about money: how to get it, how to carry it, how to change it, and how to spend it wisely. But handling money abroad is not as complicated as it used to be. These tips should help make it easy:

QUICK FIGURING

Fear of foreign currency, or lack of respect for it, is what causes travelers to waste a lot of it. Those peculiar bills and coins look like play money, and they just don't seem as important as the dollars you paid for them. Vendors are aware of this, and many are prepared to take advantage. But if you keep your wits about you, this trap can be avoided.

Carry a small calculator. The credit-card type is best. Note the exchange rate when you enter a country. The exchange offices at borders, as well as most banks, post the rates prominently every day, listing all of the major currencies. In Holland, for example, the board might say, "$1 = 1.92." Divide $1.00 by 1.92 and you'll find that one guilder equals $.52. Then when you shop, bear in mind that the ratio is roughly two guilders to the U.S. dollar. This way you will have some idea how much "real money" you are actually being charged.

MONEY FROM HOME

When you need extra funds far from home, it's now hardly ever a problem, thanks to the international monetary system. Electronic banking makes it as easy as at the ATM at home.

CREDIT CARDS

If you have a major credit card, you can walk into a bank in almost any country and walk out with a fistful of the local legal tender. In many countries you can choose your currency. It is charged to your account in dollars at the rate prevailing at the time of the transaction. The most widely accepted card by far is VISA, followed by Mastercard. American Express is primarily useful for the free bathrooms at their offices.

In Great Britain, Denmark, France, Germany, and Sweden, some banks have automatic teller machines (ATMs) that supposedly will give you a cash advance on your VISA card (known as "Carte Bleu" in France), and sometimes on your MasterCard. The cards must be properly encoded. Ask your issuing bank at home to add a *foreign code* to the card. It will then work not only in the above-mentioned countries, but also in New Zealand, Singapore, and South Africa—theoretically.

But beware! These machines check electronically with your home bank before issuing cash. If your bank is closed, they may keep your card until it opens again. Check the time before trying this. If the European banks are open, go inside and get your money the old-fashioned way.

Credit cards are widely used in Europe; you can use them to buy food at many supermarkets and gasoline at many stations, and you can often pay highway tolls with them. They're fast replacing traveler's cheques as the way to carry money.

TRAVELER'S CHEQUES

Few shops and restaurants arc willing to accept these. They are not regarded as currency by most merchants. They will often ask you to take them to a bank and bring back some cash. This can be inconvenient, but it makes them a safe way to carry money.

In Hungary, bank clerks will look puzzled and annoyed, discuss it with their superiors, and then send you not very courteously to IBUSZ, the tourist bureau, to cash your traveler's cheques.

Thomas Cook cheques can be cashed at their various offices throughout Europe free of charge, which makes them a good buy if you don't mind the search.

WIRING MONEY

Having your bank wire funds to a bank in Europe is a method used by some people. It's more complicated and takes longer than other methods, and is very expensive. We tried it in Switzerland, where they know a thing or two about banking. It took ten days. This was not due to errors or inefficiency, but to banking procedures and holidays and weekends.

INTERNATIONAL MONEY ORDERS

These things are recommended by some travel books. Obviously, the writers never tried to cash one. We did. We do not recommend them.

THE COST OF IT ALL

WHAT YOU SHOULD PLAN TO SPEND

There are so many variables in this question, it's difficult to answer with any accuracy. The cost of your van or motorhome, of course, has a lot to do with it. If you buy a van for $5,000 with a 65 per cent buy-back, then you know that transportation and lodging are going to cost you $1,750, whether you stay for two months or a year. If you buy a $10,000 rig, that cost will be more like $3,500. A rental vehicle can cost from $200 to $1200 per week.

Fuel and food are also major expenses, and they're just as variable. An estimated average for all running expenses for two people, living comfortably, eating well and spending money intelligently, is between $1,000 and $1,500 per month, exclusive of the cost of the vehicle and airfare.

Some countries are more expensive in general than others, and your costs will depend on where you spend the most time. We've divided the countries into categories as follows:

Expensive

Austria, Germany, Great Britain, Italy, Scandinavia, Switzerland

About the same as at home

France, Holland, Spain

Inexpensive

Czech Republic, Hungary, Greece, Portugal, Turkey

Chapter 8

Bringing the Kids
(But Not the Dog)

No doubt about it, motorhoming is the way to travel with children. They have the security of a familiar bed every night, space to play while you're on the road, their own clean toilet, and the kind of food they're used to. You are spared those excruciating waits in restaurants with tired, cranky little ones, hotel rooms festooned with laundry, and worries about germs in strange bathrooms. Midday naps, potty breaks, and snack times are easily accomplished at a moment's notice by pulling into the next rest area. In the evening you can tuck them in bed and have a couple of hours of adult time in a way that you never could in a hotel.

BUT NOT THE DOG

But the family dog will have to stay at home, much as you'd like to have his enthusiastic company in the forests and meadows of Europe and the security of his presence on guard when you leave your motorhome for a few hours. The laws make it very difficult.

Great Britain requires a quarantine period of six months. Although the Netherlands and Germany will allow you to import a dog if it has had rabies shots at least thirty days and no more than one year before entry, for Germany you must have a Health and Rabies Certificate *in German* which has been certified by the U.S. Animal and Plant Health Inspection Service.

Besides, no animal you love should be subjected to a terrifying and possibly life-threatening twelve-hour flight in the baggage compartment.

PLANNING AHEAD

When you choose your motorhome there are several things to bear in mind for comfort and safety when you're traveling with children. First, be sure to get a model that is large enough. Elsewhere we've encouraged you to choose the smallest vehicle you can live with, for ease of driving and parking and for fuel economy. But unless your children are very young, a smaller van is going to be pretty snug for freecamping or rainy days. Many VWs, however, have a fold-out bed up above, or even an "upper story" that sleeps two. Small cots that can be stretched across the front passenger seats are also available for babies or toddlers. But if your kids are large and rambunctious it might be best to rent or buy a larger motorhome to allow some wiggle room.

For small children, a portable potty will save you from many a sudden emergency, although Europeans are much more tolerant than Americans of outdoor peeing—at least by males. Although we generally feel that a chemical toilet is an unnecessary accessory, in this case it may be worth the mess and loss of space.

SEAT BELTS

European laws about children and car restraints vary from country to country, but in general it is required that you and the kids buckle up at all times when you are riding in the front, and that children who are too small for regulation seat belts be confined in special infant seats. Of course you must never share a belt with a child or hold him or her on your lap while you're riding. The law is a bit vague about back seats, and even vaguer about the rear of motorhomes. For practical purposes, even if it is not required by law, you may want to have seat belts installed at the table, so the kids can have a play or drawing surface while they ride safely. It is highly unlikely that you will find a van or motorhome that is already equipped with rear belts.

WHAT TO PACK FOR KIDS

If you're renting your motorhome, you may not need to bring along any dishes or linens or sleeping bags unless the kids have emotional attachments to a certain cup or blanket. Check ahead with your rental company to see how many of these items they are willing to supply.

When you pack the toys, a mixture of a few old, familiar things and some new surprises is a wise choice. Choose toys that have lots of play possibilities, like a small doll with interesting changes of clothes and accessories, or a set of small trucks and cars. Spiral-bound drawing pads with colored pencils are good for hours of fun, but don't bring crayons, which melt in the sun (or in a van left in the sun). Toys with hundreds of small pieces (Lego is the classic example) can be a constant annoyance in a small living space unless your child is an exceptional picker-upper. But bear in mind, when you consider buying surprises for the trip, that almost all the quality toys for young children that are sold in America are made in Germany or the Netherlands, so it may be better (and cheaper) to wait and buy things as you go. We have noticed that children who are *not* surrounded with piles of toys get very creative in finding ways to have fun with whatever random objects they find on the trip.

GETTING READY

Older children and teenagers will enjoy the trip more, and so will you, if you do your homework ahead of time—but for goodness sake, don't call it that ("Is this a vacation or a field trip?" asked one lippy teen). Leave interesting brochures and folders lying around, and talk to your mate in glowing terms about the historical and natural wonders you'll be seeing—within hearing of the kids. Ask your librarian for suggestions of books your kids will like that describe the places you'll be visiting. Try to include the kids' interests when you're planning the itinerary. Ask them—they may surprise you.

A consulting service to help families plan and prepare

for trips is offered by an organization called "Travelling With Children," 2313 Valley St., Berkeley, CA 94702. The owners, Dan and Wendy Hallinan, have accumulated a wealth of information in their own world travels with their three children. For an appointment phone (510) 848-0929, fax (510) 848-0935. The fee for a consultation is $25 plus phone charges, but if they book your entire trip, including airfare, there is no charge.

Take Your Kids To Europe by Cynthia Harriman (1994, $15.00 ppd.) is a very helpful book. It's available from Mason-Grant Publications, 57 South St., Portsmouth, NH 03801, Tel (603) 436-1608.

CAMPGROUNDS AND KIDS

When you're at last on the road, and you arrive in a campground, you can safely let older kids run, with a few precautions. Make sure they know the route back to "home" from the playground and the toilets. Many camps are large and confusing, and all motorhomes can begin to look alike to a scared and lost child. If your kids are new to camping, teach them how to stay on the beaten path and not violate the invisible boundaries of other people's "front yards." You'll probably find that your kids make friends right away, regardless of language barriers. One of the great and amazing sights of European travel is watching a group of children communicate perfectly when they share not one word in common.

DIVIDING UP CHORES

Kids will feel more a part of the whole enterprise if they have regular tasks on the trip. To help make the morning routine go more quickly, younger children can put dirty clothes in the laundry bag, tie back the curtains, empty the trash, while older kids can sweep the floor and wipe the dust or dew off the windshield. You can even make a game of seeing how quickly you can get on the road after breakfast.

While you're driving, older children and teens can be entrusted with navigating from the map and reading aloud interesting bits from the guidebook, or keeping records of expenditures and computing gas mileage. Kids old enough to read the guidebook should also have a democratic hand in deciding which points of interest they think *they* would find of interest.

SIGHTS WITH HIGH "KID APPEAL"

Europe is so rich with wonderful things to see that you should have no trouble choosing. Simple things may delight little children the most, like chunking rocks in a lake or feeding ducks (but watch out for geese and swans—they can get mean when the food supply is all gone). It is important to keep your pace leisurely to give children time to enjoy on their own level, and to vary your activities from day to day. What teenagers like best of all is fast food and other teens, in that order. Nevertheless, here for starters is a brief selection of some kinds of European sights that kids may find particularly great.

MUSEUMS

Of course *you* want to go to the Louvre and the Prado and the Uffizi. Kids may or may not come along willingly to these high-class experiences, but what they would really like might be found in Europe's many special museums. The barrel organ museum in Utrecht,

Holland, for instance, which has all kinds of amazing and ornate automatic music machines that really play. Or the nautical museum near Oslo, Norway, where you can see restored Viking ships. Or the fashion museum in Paris. Or the grisly Black Museum or Madame Tussaud's Waxworks in London. Or the wind-up toy museum in Munich. Or the Deutsches Museum, also in that city, which has large sections devoted to the history of machinery and transportation, including a walk-through U-boat from World War II and all kinds of things that chug and whir.

CAR MUSEUMS

These abound, and automotive-minded kids will be agog at models and styles they have never seen before. Some good ones are at Sinsheim and Amerang, Germany, Mulhouse and Le Mans, France, and Ramsgate, England.

OPEN-AIR MUSEUMS

The idea here is to recreate the daily life of the past. Whole villages are meticulously reassembled and furnished with objects from olden times, and the town is brought to life by people dressed in the costumes of the period who demonstrate old crafts and skills. You can spend hours wandering through these magical places, making discoveries around every corner and through every doorway. The oldest is Skansen, near Stockholm, but others the kids will like are the Zuidersee Open-Air Museum at Enkhuizen in Holland, which is approached by boat, or Den Fynske Landsby in Odense, Denmark, where you can see a play from Hans Christian Andersen's tales here in his home town. Little children may prefer miniature villages, like Madurodam in The

Hague or Legoland in Denmark.

SPORTS

Baseball and American football are out for the duration of the trip, but if your kids like soccer you're all set. Europe abounds with opportunities to participate in and view all kinds of sports. Even playing catch or frisbee in the park is a great way to get the wiggles out, and swimming, whether in the sea, a lake, or a municipal pool, is everybody's favorite. Or you might pick up a couple of second-hand bicycles in Amsterdam, lash them onto the back of your motorhome, and use them for exploring the countryside and villages after you've settled into a campground.

CASTLES AND PALACES

Fantasy fans will be delighted to explore any and all of Europe's thousands of castles. The famous ones tend to be heavily restored and even more heavily touristed. It's more fun to find your own ruins to climb around in; every town has a crumbling castle at the top of the hill. If you read a short book on castles before you leave home (try the children's department of your public libarary), your imagination will be better able to work with what you see.

On the other hand, palaces, like cathedrals, are a big bore for kids after the first "oh, wow!" wears off.

ANIMAL PLACES

Zoos, of course, appeal to kids of all ages, and Europe has some great ones. We particularly like the nocturnal house at the Frankfurt Zoo. Aquariums, too, are sure fire pleasures for children. The best is the one founded by Jacques Costeau in Monaco. Other animal parks are devoted to one species, like the Shetland Pony Park in Slagharen, Holland.

CIRCUSES AND OTHER SUCH PERFORMANCES

If you run across a circus, you're in luck. These are delightfully intimate compared to the New World version. You can see the expressions on the clowns' faces and almost touch the tigers and lions. Circus Knie out of Switzerland is a great one. Street performers are found in many cities, especially outside the Pompidou in Paris, at Covent Garden in London, and at the Marienplatz in Munich. Kids will love the jugglers, magicians, and mimes. Be sure to let them put money in the hat afterward. For a special treat, budding ballerinas will be thrilled by a ballet performance in an elegant opera house.

SEMI-SCARY EXPERIENCES

Both kids and adults like to be scared—a little bit. Cave tours are just shivery enough. The best part, of course, is the pitch-black moment when they turn out all the lights. Funiculars and chair lifts are deliciously breathtaking. An especially exciting one ascends Gibraltar, with stops to visit the Barbary apes.

THEME PARKS

As in North America, these are expensive, but a powerful incentive for good behavior. Tivoli, in Copenhagen, is the grandaddy of them all, although kids who have been to Disneyland (for which it was the inspiration) may find its charm a bit underwhelming. More modern parks are the brand new Futurescope near Poitiers,

France, and Asterix, outside of Paris, which is based on the comic strip. The big one, of course, is Euro Disney, also near Paris.

The Carousel in the gardens of Versailles. (Photo by David Shore)

Chapter 9

Staying Safe and Healthy:
Feel-Good Tips

In general, you should have no trouble staying well and happy on your trip, if you observe a few common sense rules. You may even feel better than at home, with all that walking, outdoor living, good food, and the excitement of beautiful sights and new ideas.

ON-THE-ROAD HEALTH BASICS

Certain precautions should be part of every traveler's bag of tricks. We take a thousand milligrams a day of Vitamin C on the road, and we've noticed that the only time we ever get sick on a trip is when we run out. Bring a supply with you, because Europeans consider it a medicine and consequently it is sold in very small quantities for high prices. Go easy on new foods until your stomach gets over being surprised, but otherwise you don't need to take any special precautions about what you eat or drink. The tap water is perfectly safe almost everywhere, except in Southern Italy and parts of Bulgaria, Poland and Romania. Occasionally a campground may have separate faucets for potable and nonpotable water; the one marked with a picture of a drinking glass and a slash is, obviously, nonpotable. Otherwise you should be able to drink with impunity, unless you do something silly like filling your water bottle from an ornamental fountain or a river. Remember that when you swim in a lake or sea, you're drinking it if you swallow water—and swans are picturesque but polluting.

EXERCISE

Getting enough exercise is not a problem when you're sightseeing, but be sure to wear comfortable shoes for all that walking. We always find that we arrive home ten pounds thinner after a three-month trip, in spite of all the good eating. However, you may find yourself in need of stretching when you spend several days on the road; an amusing solution is to find a children's playground after dark and have a swing on the monkeybars. If you like to jog in the morning, you'll have plenty of company in city parks or country back roads. In Northern European countries you may even find an occasional "fitness park" with a course laid out among stations with various kinds of exercise ladders and bars.

JET LAG

Before you can feel good you have to get over the inevitable jet lag. This is not a serious health hazard, but it can be disorienting for the first three or four days. Recently a number of articles and books have offered elaborate schemes for overcoming the effects, mostly by turning your life upside-down for a week before you leave. We find all this more trouble than it's worth. Flying from North America you'll be six to nine hours out of sync (depending on where you start from), and this is distressing for your body no matter what you do. We find it takes us at least four days to recover (which is one reason we do not take two-week tours of Europe).

It helps to know that the exhaustion, loss of appetite, and feelings of unreality that you're experiencing are normal and temporary. Don't blame the way you're feeling on Europe or your partner. Just take it easy at first. Don't force yourself to eat, take naps only when you must, and try to get into the new diurnal rhythm as soon as you can. As a motorhome traveler, you have no pressing schedules to meet, so go to a campground and rest for a day or two while you adjust. Don't launch into strenuous sightseeing or driving immediately. Reality will soon come back into focus and you can be off with renewed energy.

DOCTORS AND MEDICINE

All European countries have some sort of government-subsidized medical care, but they don't always allow visitors to benefit from it. In general, doctors and medicine will be cheaper than at home if you should need them while you're abroad. Nevertheless, it is a good idea to check with your medical insurer at home before you leave, to find out their rules for overseas reimbursement and to fortify yourself with the necessary forms and papers. Kaiser Permanente, for instance, will pay only on life-threatening emergencies, and you must notify them within 48 hours of the occurence and have the proper claim forms with you. Under normal conditions, extra travelers' health insurance is necessary only for those with chronic health problems.

Take an adequate supply of any prescription drugs you may need. The chemicals and the rules may be different in Europe. Asthma inhalators, for instance, are not sold over the counter. On the other hand, some kinds of medical care may be better; Patty always has her glasses ground and fitted in Germany, for example.

PEDESTRIAN SAFETY

"What's the most dangerous trick you've done this evening?" we once asked a juggler in Amsterdam. Putting away his torches and swords, he didn't hesitate.

"Crossing the tram tracks," he shot back.

Crossing the street *can* be hazardous to your health in European cities. The traffic is very fast and aggressive, and cars dart in and out of lanes without warning. Streetcars (or "trams") come from unexpected directions. Add to that the complication of the many bicycles and motorbikes, and you've got a situation that calls for constant vigilance every time you step off the curb. This is especially true in Great Britain, where it's all coming at you from the wrong direction. In England, Scotland, and Ireland remind yourself frequently to "Look right!" when you get ready to cross.

FIRE SAFETY

Inside your motorhome we want to warn you to be super-careful with fire. When we were novice vanners, we used to think it was romantic to have candlelit dinners—until the night David leaned across the table for a kiss and sat back with his hair in a crown of flames. From the candle, not the kiss. Luckily, we got the fire smothered before he was burned, but ever since we have been very aware of fire safety.

Please be sure to tie your curtains well away from the stove when you are cooking, and be careful not to let hot fat ignite in the pan. If this should ever happen, don't throw water on it; smother it with a lid. Don't wear trailing scarves or mufflers or loose sleeves when you're the cook, and never lay paper napkins or paper towels near the fire. Always open the window a bit when you light the burner to prevent carbon monoxide buildup—even when it's cold outside. And never use the stove for heat while you sleep.

MOSQUITOES AND OTHER BUGS

After all these dire warnings, it's something of an anticlimax to talk about insects, but a good crop of mosquito bites can be pretty uncomfortable. Not to speak of a night's sleep lost because of their infernal whine. Prevention is the cure. When you buy or rent your van, tight screens are a definite plus, although not a feature you can always find. Be aware when you choose a spot for the night that these pesky critters breed not only in marshy places, but also in trash piles. (Once we had a persistent swarm of the things every night, no matter where we stopped and how carefully we checked our screens for holes. We finally figured out that they were emerging from some figs we had home-dried and stored in the cupboard.) As soon as the sun goes down protect yourself by rubbing on a good repellent. Autan is an effective brand in Europe, but any product containing a high percentage of N-diethyltoluamide (DEET) will do.

In a sidewalk cafe, a streak of Autan on the table on both sides of the plate keeps flies away from your lunch. But be discreet when you do it, so as not to offend the waiter.

CLEAN AND NEAT

Good housekeeping in the motorhome is important for mental health, and the smaller the rig the more essential this is. Empty the trash and wash the dishes before you go to bed; otherwise that pan of cold grease and onions is going to be just inches away from your nose while you try to sleep. Sweep up the crumbs and sand from the floor before you get on the road every morning, and swab out the sink after you brush your teeth. Hose the dust off the outside occasionally when you hit a campground with a car-washing area. Making a habit of all these small moves will keep your self-respect up.

For peaceful van living, neatness and organization are essential, even if that's not your natural style, and again, the smaller the rig, the more vital this is. The alternative is an uncomfortable crowded mess, where everything is in your way and you can never find anything. Don't bring a single thing with you from home that you don't absolutely need. When you pick up your rental motorhome, look over the kitchen equipment and leave everything you don't think you'll use with the rental office. The day you move in to your camper, agree together on a place for each category: clothes (mine and yours), shoes, dirty laundry, toiletries, dishes, food, books, maps, sports equipment, etc. Then always put things away as soon as you're through with them.

Try to stow everything so that there is nothing you repeatedly have to climb over and shift around. Remember to bring only soft luggage you can fold up flat to store. Don't buy big bulky items on the trip unless you can have them mailed home immediately or pick them up later near the end of your travels. One couple we know almost ruined their relationship over a large gift box of copper cookware that crowded their van unbearably for a month.

THE VAN CHOREOGRAPHY

If you and your travelmate have never lived together in a motorhome, it will take a couple of days of shakedown before everything goes smoothly. You must move slowly and predictably and telegraph your moves verbally at first.

Say "I need to reach and get the map out of that cupboard over your head," or "I'm going to pour this boiling water in the cup now" before you do it.

Staying Safe And Healthy

It helps to get into a rhythm and a pattern at possible friction points. For instance, at bedtime one partner can have the whole space to wash and undress, while the other reads in a corner out of the way. Then they can put the bed down together; the first partner can climb in, and the other can have a turn at the washing and undressing space. In the morning, you can reverse the process, with the difference that the first riser goes for a short walk after dressing to give the second more room. Agree on a division of the routine breakfast and clean-up tasks in the morning so you can get on the road quickly without discussion.

A technique that works for us is borrowed from the Japanese knack for creating psychological distance in crowded circumstances. When one of us needs a moment of privacy, we say, "Please go in the other room." Then the partner is obligated to turn around, stare out the window or at the wall, and mentally absent himself or herself for the necessary amount of time, until called back. It may sound silly, but this small piece of courtesy is an effective way to create privacy.

Living together happily in a motorhome or van draws on all the skills of maintaining a good relationship, but on an intensified level. Be aware of the other person's need for space, both physical and psychological, and give a bit more than you think your partner needs. People vary in their requirements for lebensraum. A large person, obviously, will need leg and elbow room, but a physically small person with an expansive personality might need more space than a large quiet partner. The taller vanmate (whether male or female) should be careful not to sprawl out all over the seat so that the other person has to curl up in a cramped corner. Men tend to be less aware than women when they are violating someone

else's personal territory, and women tend to fume silent-
ly when they are imposed upon.

Watch out for irritating habits in yourself—tapping,
whistling, hair-twirling. These can escalate at close
quarters into major annoyances. More assertive people
should be careful not to thoughtlessly impose their pref-
erences about music, radio stations, and bedtime on
gentler partners. A willingness to speak up as soon as
something bothers you is necessary, and discussion and
compromise are important tools. All this is excellent
practice for general compatibility as well as happy
motorhome living, and you may go home with your relationship in better shape than when you arrived.

HOMESICKNESS

Embarrassing as it is to admit, little kids at summer
camp are not the only people who get homesick.
Grownups on a long trip in a foreign land can come
down with it, too. Prolonged culture shock can once in a
while bring on that hollow, sad feeling unexpectedly.
Sometimes the remedy is just a telephone call home to
make sure everything is all right. Other times a bit of
Americana is just what's needed. Tapes of down-home
music like country/western or pop rock may do it for
some people; others prefer Golden Oldies—just so long
as it's unmistakably sounds from home. We carry several tapings of Garrison Keillor's dear departed radio pro-
gram, "A Prairie Home Companion" for just such
emergencies. Or you might read aloud from Mark Twain
or Erma Bombeck. Or perhaps you might be comforted
by cooking yourself some soul food like pork chops and
mashed potatoes with gravy.

MAKING FRIENDS

After the crisis is over, the real remedy for culture shock is to get more deeply into the pace and style of the place where you are. Socializing and making friends will give you affectionate insights into foreign ways. Some of our most treasured experiences have come from being guests in European homes, and from long talks with our hosts in which we learned that, while our differences were interesting, our similiarities were basic.

VAN AND MOTORHOME SECURITY

Europe is not a very dangerous place compared to the U.S. Violence is not equated with fun there, the way it is in America. Europeans have been through a couple of world wars, and they've had enough. War toys are not often seen in the toy shops, especially in Germany. In Munich a bombed-out building still stands unrestored among the glittering new structures. Across its fractured facade are painted the words "KRIEG NIE WIEDER"— "War never again." Violence is abhorrent to most Europeans, and violent crimes are relatively rare. In fact, many Europeans say that they are afraid to visit the U.S.

We travel without fear or worry. We keep a healthy awareness, however, of the dangers of complacency, and we use a bit of common sense and a few precautions.

Once these precautions are understood, they become second nature. After reading this chapter, discuss it with your traveling companion and work out how you will adapt these recommendations to your own situations. Then go forth with confidence and peace of mind, knowing that common sense will be your guide. Those who prey on "easy marks" will have to look elsewhere.

They're over by the tour bus anyway.

We've put together a list of precautions that will help you maintain security and enjoy a vacation free of the kind of unpleasant experiences we sometimes hear about from returning tourists. You won't have any such stories to tell if you heed this checklist:

SECURITY CHECKLIST

Take These Precautions, Then Relax

1. *Don't be paranoid.* Trust people. Remember that Europe is a safer place than the U.S.

2. *Install a burglar alarm.* Visibly, even if you don't bother to connect it.

3. *Park wisely.* Avoid dark, secluded places, especially if you see broken auto glass.

4. *Always lock your vehicle.*

5. *Never leave valuables in view.* They're open invitations. Take your camera with you.

6. *Carry a set of car keys with each of you.* And don't leave them both unguarded on the beach when you go swimming.

7. *Keep your wallet on your person.* In a safe place, not in your back pocket. And remember to close your purse between purchases.

Staying Safe And Healthy

8. *Keep your passport and credit cards separate from your wallet.* In another secure pocket or in a zipper compartment in your purse.

9. *Carry travelers' cheques and as little cash as possible.* Or use your credit card to draw cash as you go.

10. *Carry a big secure purse.* With zippered compartments, and shoulder straps that can reach across your chest to foil snatchers on motorbikes. In cafes, hang it over your knee, never on the back of the chair.

11. *Women, never walk alone in isolated places at night.* Basic common sense anywhere in the world.

12. *Don't act like a tourist.* A loud voice and a superior manner will mark you as the Ugly American, a target ripe for a rip-off.

Organization is important in small vans. (Photo by David Shore)

Large kitchen with raised fridge

Chapter 10

Cooking On Wheels:
Healthy, Cheap, and Fun

WHY COOK?

So why, you say, should I cook on this vacation? Well, let us say right off that if you have plenty of money, excellent digestion, will only be on the road for two or three weeks, and have always considered cooking a boring chore, probably you shouldn't. Under any other circumstances there are lots of good reasons for planning to cook at least some of your meals in your motorhome.

First, eating three times a day in restaurants can be extremely expensive in some countries. Perhaps economizing is not important to you, but even if I were a billionaire my Scottish soul would balk at the $22 cafe owners wanted for a small ordinary pizza in Italy recently. Groceries, on the other hand, usually run about the same price or lower than at home.

Second, a steady diet of high-calorie, high-fat restaurant food is bad for your health, and total immersion in exotic cuisines can have equally exotic effects on your digestion. And it's much easier to control dietary requirements like low sodium if you're the cook.

Third, shopping for your daily bread puts you in touch with the culture. You're out there admiring the local peaches or enjoying the smell of fresh rolls while you wait your turn at the bakery, just like the folks who live there. It helps you understand what's what in a country.

Fourth, being prepared to cook gives you greater flexibility. You can get on the road faster in the morning, picnic under a tree or beside a castle at a whim, have a comforting cup of hot soup on a rainy day without getting your feet wet. When evening comes, you can pull into a rest area for the night whenever you get tired, or stay an extra day at a lovely beach, or watch the moon rise over remote Grecian ruins—if you have the fixings for dinner.

Last—and this is the most important reason—it's fun to cook in a motorhome. Sort of like playing doll house when you were a kid. European groceries can be glorious, and shopping for them is a game full of interesting surprises. Anyone who likes to cook at all will have a wonderful time playing with all the gourmet goodies to be found for pennies on the Continent. You'll soon come to feel sorry for those poor tourists who can't do anything but *look* in the street markets and the cheese and wine shops.

YOUR ROLLING KITCHEN

So, back in the van kitchen, it's time to get ready to cook. Let's take a look at your equipment. Your built-in stove will have two burners, but no broiler or oven unless you've got a real luxury rig. It will use propane, which is a vast improvement over those smelly, noisy kerosene camp cookers which used to need endless pumping and would make your pans all sooty. Propane is clean, quiet, and lights instantly. It is sold in camping supply shops in towns and at the campground store under the brand name "Camping Gaz." The blue metal bottles come in four sizes, but the little ones are not worth bothering with. Your first bottle can be expensive

Cooking on Wheels

(as much as $30) but motorhome rental companies and dealers will usually provide it free for their customers. Screw it onto the attachment pipe and it will fuel your stove for about a month if you're cooking every day; you can tell you're running low when the flame begins to turn orange instead of blue. Then exchange it for a refilled bottle, which should cost somewhere between $4 and $20. Obviously, it pays to time it so that you run out in a cheap country. A spare is nice to have for peace of mind if you have room to store it.

If you have a refrigerator, it will also run on propane when you're standing still. When you're traveling it can often be switched over to the car battery—which is a great saving. A refrigerator is pleasant to have, but not as absolutely essential as we Americans think. The technique is to shop frequently, snuggle the meat and milk up to the water bottle, and throw away leftovers. And learn to love warm beer. Block ice or ice cubes are unobtainable in Europe but you can get those blue plastic fake-ice things and sometimes it is possible to freeze them at a campground..

Your motorhome should also have a sink with faucet and drain, supplied with water from a plastic bottle underneath. Five gallons lasts us three days, and then we fill up at a campground or gas station or highway rest stop. Water is almost always safe for drinking, but we usually take the precaution at a gas station to ask "Po*ta*ble?"—a word which is generally understood. If the water is not okay in campground and rest stops there will be a sign showing a drinking glass with a slash through it. Needless to say, don't ever fill your water bottle at streams or lakes, no matter how remote. In a van your sink drain may empty right out on the ground, so it is respectful of other people and the environment to carry a bucket you can put under the pipe when you stop for the night.

TOOLS TO BRING

What cooking equipment should you give space in your luggage? A well-stocked motorhome kitchen should have the following essentials:

- A bottle opener (the kind called a "church key")
- A hook bottle opener
- A corkscrew
- A can opener
- A big slicing knife, not serrated
- A small paring knife
- Extra knives, forks, and spoons (in case of guests)
- Two tablespoons
- A small spatula
- A grater
- Coffee cups as needed
- Sturdy wine glasses as needed
- Plates as needed
- A medium-sized pot with a lid and double handles rather than a handle that sticks out
- A cast-iron skillet (worth the weight) and a lid of some lighter material
- A coffee filter cone, if you deplore instant

And if you have room you might also bring:

- Soup bowls as needed
- A second pot
- A little cutting board

This may seem like a lot, written out in a list, but actually it all packs into a quite small space. Or this basic equipment can be picked up cheaply at a flea market when you arrive, or supplemented with pieces you buy just for fun on the road. We are especially fond of the black and red enamel pot we found in Yugoslavia (actually Patty knocked it off the shelf and cracked the handle so we had to buy it) and our earthenware tapa dishes from Spain—not to speak of the set of tiny steel teaspoons we collected one at a time from highway franchise restaurants.

Many dealers and rental agencies will provide complete kitchen equipment—often more than you need. Check on this before you leave home, if you've made arrangements ahead for your vehicle. In any case, you may still want to bring your favorite knife or coffee cup.

SETTLING INTO YOUR MINI-KITCHEN

When you move into your newly acquired motorhome or van, your first housekeeping job after putting everything away in all the clever little cupboards and storage spaces is to go out and buy a few staples. Taking it easy on yourself because of jet lag, find a supermarket and pick up:

- Salt and pepper
- Any other spices you use often
- Oil
- Sugar or honey
- Coffee and/or tea
- Dishwashing liquid
- Sponge with scouring side
- Paper towels
- Hand soap

If your dealer has not provided them, also buy a plastic bucket in a size you can store under the seat and a short-handled sweep-up brush. Now, as soon as you rig up a holder for the paper towels your rolling kitchen is ready for action.

MEAL PLANS

Take a tip from the Europeans and keep breakfast simple: cold ham and cheese, cereal or a boiled egg, fresh fruit, or a sampling of local breads. Who wants to start a day on the road with a greasy skillet to wash?

Lunch, of course, should be a picnic (or a bowl of hot soup if it's raining). Lovely spots abound when you've got wheels, and the cheese and pate and pastries are the stuff of romantic dreams.

One daytime situation where you might overlook the need for preparation is ferry crossings. These always involve long waiting in line. When you do finally drive onto the boat you'll probably be starving, but the eating counters and cafeterias on these vessels can be skimpy and uninspired, and they are always wildly expensive (with the exception of the Sally Line's famous brunch on the English Channel crossing). Think ahead, and buy a few goodies before you are trapped in line so you can picnic on deck in the fresh breeze and admire the passing scenery.

Dinner is the only meal for which you need to do any real cooking. Sometimes all you'll want to do is bring home the yummies from the charcuterie or deli and spread them out decoratively. Other times you'll want to get more creative. Our menus center around an instant appetizer, one interesting hot dish, and a simple salad. Desserts we leave to the experts: Just choose from the counter of the nearest bakery. Or conduct a serious comparative study of the many delectable European chocolate bars.

International Breakfasts

People feel strongly everywhere about the appropriate food to eat first thing in the morning. Each country has a pattern that everybody considers the normal, logical breakfast, and any food ideas that stray too far from the pattern are considered peculiar, or even nauseating. We've noticed that if people can't get their own cultural breakfast in foreign countries they tend to get grumpy. We hope you're more flexible and will give a try to:

Smoked fish, cheese, dark bread, and coffee in Scandinavia

Fried eggs and tomatoes, bacon, toast, tea in England

Salami, liverwurst, and other cold cuts, hard and soft
    cheese, butter, jam, chocolate spread, two or
    three kinds of bread, coffee in Germany

Soft-boiled eggs and thin-sliced cold ham and cheese,
    several kinds of bread, coffee in Holland

Store-bought toast, biscuits or rolls with soft cheese
    spreads and capuchin in Italy

Bread or churros (long crisp doughnuts) and coffee in
    Spain

Feta cheese and hard cheese, bread in hunks, butter and
    jam, Greek olives, sliced tomatoes, tea in Turkey

Cafe au lait and a croissant in France

But you'll probably want to decline the espresso washed down
    with a glass of slivovitz which many Yugoslavs use to get
    their day into high gear.

EFFICIENT COOKING TECHNIQUES

To cook well in a van or small motorhome, you must move slowly and predictably and you must think through before you move. A lack of forethought can lead to chaos and hot spills at close quarters.

The first step is to hunker down by the cupboard and get out everything you're going to use. Don't forget the salt or the silverware or the lid for the pot. Set out a bag for peelings and trash and go to work. As you finish with each item, slip it back into the cupboard if you can reach it easily. As a pan or dish is emptied, set it in the sink to soak. By the time you're ready to serve the main course, the table should be clear except for silverware, plates, and napkins.

Afterward, if you've been faithful to the Goddess of Order, you'll have only one pot and a knife and your silverware and plates and wine glasses to wash—a snap. Put the water on to heat while you drink your coffee, and then a quick squirt of detergent, a swish with the sponge, a rinse with boiling water, and you're all done. After a couple of days the whole procedure becomes automatic, leaving you only the enjoyment.

Chapter 11

Food Shopping:
Another Facet of Europe

We now approach the adventure of going out in a strange country and buying food to cook in your motorhome. To begin with, forget most of what you already know about camp cooking. No canned beans and franks or toasted marshmallows. No bonfire either. What we are talking about here is exploring the little shops and open-air marketplaces of Europe and bringing home to your rig the freshest, most delicate of what you find there. We're talking about preparing it quickly and simply and enjoying a comfortable, civilized dinner with music and wine. We're talking about exploring new culinary delights, finding new dimensions in familiar foods, revelling in goodies you could never get at home.

On this trip you'll find you need and want to shop for food as you go along every day, mainly because it's more fun that way. When you pass an intriguing pastry shop or a great-smelling wurst stand or a bustling open-air market, don't promise yourself to come back in the late afternoon when you're in the mood to think about dinner. You may be miles away. Stop right then for the moment or two it takes to buy those goodies, then tuck them in your daypack and proceed with your sightseeing. You'll be glad later.

The Viktualien Markt, Munich.

OUTDOOR MARKETS

A delightful type of shopping that you will experience nearly everywhere in Europe is the open-air market. These are social events as much as places, and they usually happen only once a week in any particular location (although some famous markets in large cities are held daily). Stalls are set up in a public square or down both sides of a main street or in and around a central market hall. Wednesday, Friday, and Saturday are favorite days, and morning is the best time to shop; by two o'clock the merchants have usually started to pack away and sweep up. Everything is dewy fresh and often locally produced. You'll find beautiful fruits and vegetables, but also often eggs, honey, olives, cheese, and sausage. Take your time and stroll through the whole market, comparing quality and prices and enjoying the scene. Except in Britain, the prices will be by the kilo (kg) and will seem high until you figure out that a kilo is about two pounds. What you will probably want is a half kilo, or a "demi." Bargaining is usually not the custom; you pay what is asked.

The written European-style numbers can be confusing to American eyes. If it's a seven, it will have a short horizontal stroke across the stem. If it looks like a seven but lacks the cross-stroke, it is a one.

Two more very important pieces of know-how: never handle the produce, though you can point to the items you want. Only the largest supermarkets allow you to pick out your own vegetables and put them in a sack, but even there you must take them to a self-service automatic scale or a produce clerk to be weighed and labeled before you get in the checkout line. Second, bring your own bag. Save the plastic ones from the supermarket or carry a fold-up nylon carry-all. A basket is romantic if you have room in your rig to store it.

SHOPPING COMMUNICATION TECHNIQUE

Wonderful eats can also be found in the small bakeries and butcher and pastry shops. But what about language? Surprisingly, this is not usually a problem, as we explained in Chapter VI. You will often find that the person behind the counter speaks excellent English, especially in Northern Europe.

If this turns out not to be the case, a smile and gestures go a long way toward bridging the communication gap. Just point, and say please in the local idiom, and the salesperson will say something back that logic will tell you means, "How much do you want?" If it's slices you're after, pantomime cutting with a stiff hand across your other palm, and then hold up fingers to show how many. If you only indicate the number with fingers there will inevitably be some confusion about whether you want that many slices or that many kilos. If the substance you're buying can be cut in hunks or scooped up in a measure, use your fingers to show how big a piece or your cupped hands to show how much. And so on. You may feel silly, but it works.

WEIGHTS AND CHANGE

As in the produce market, prices are by the kilo, or (if what you're buying is likely to be eaten in small quantities) in grams. One hundred grams is the standard size for one large or two small servings, and sometimes the posted price will be for that amount. When it comes time to pay, ask with gestures to have the words written down in numerals if there is no cash register to read. In case of total confusion simply hold out a palmful of miscellaneous coins and throw yourself on their mercy. We find that shopkeepers will always respond by counting out the change very slowly and carefully so you can see that they are not cheating you.

SUPERMARKETS

In a supermarket, of course, there is no such folksy interchange. Everything is modern and efficient, especially in the gigantic super-supermarkets called hypermarches. You may be tempted to take this easy way out, and sometimes it makes sense when you're in a hurry or are stocking up on staples. Or out of cash—many hypermarches take Visa or Mastercard.

But be forewarned that even in the biggest stores

you'll be expected to bag your own groceries—and you'd better be quick about it or the next person's order will come sliding into yours. If you want bags, you must ask for them and sometimes you will be charged.

Another difference from North American supermarkets is that you must take your fruits and vegetables to the weighing machine in the produce section, where, if there is no attendant, you put each sack on the scale and push the button with the picture of the fruit or vegetable. A gummed label with the price will magically appear; stick it securely on the bag to close it.

In some countries you must "rent" your shopping cart by inserting a small coin in a slot on the handle to release a chain. When you're through shopping and have unloaded the cart, plug the chain back in and your coin will pop out.

CLOSING HOURS AND OTHER CAUTIONS

Confusion about closing hours can lead to much more shopping frustration than language differences. In Europe, when closing time comes, they close. And don't bother trying to find an all night mini-market to bail you out. Not only do all the shops (and banks and laundromats and everything else) close up at five or six, they also shut up tight at noon, not to reopen until two o'clock, or—in some southern countries—until the sun goes down. The one exception to mid-day closing is the hypermarche, but even they are silent and locked on Sunday.

Long lunch can be annoying, but Sunday closing can be disastrous if it catches you unaware. If you don't buy enough food and drink on Saturday morning to last the weekend, you're going to find yourself on Sunday evening wandering hungrily down street after deserted street looking for a place to buy something, anything, to eat.

There are two places where you should never buy groceries unless there is absolutely no other alternative: the campground store and the shops affiliated with the rest stops on the motorways. The quality and selection will be abysmal and tourist-oriented, and the prices will be appropriately high for the captive audience they think you are.

SOME GENERAL DIFFERENCES IN EUROPEAN FOODSTUFFS

Dairy products are superb everywhere in Northern Europe. Cheese, of course, is legendary, but the butter and yogurt are also great. Milk comes in two modes: fresh and sterilized (sometimes called "longlife milk"). The latter lasts a long time without souring, but has a caramelized smell. In Southern Europe, we recommend that you substitute olive oil for butter.

Produce is varied and wonderfully fresh in the open markets, but don't expect to find anything out of season. Endive and Japanese eggplant and shallots and such are luxuries that are not too costly in Europe. You will seldom find yams, corn on the cob, or the kinds of melons we're used to. Peaches and berries and grapes are swell, but citrus is not up to California standards. One uniquely European vegetable that is handy for motorhome cooking is a miniature garden of sprouts growing in a little box on wet cotton. You cut it off with scissors as you need it.

If you eat meat, veal, lamb, and ham are good almost everywhere, and pork depends on where you are. Beef is better in North America, and so is chicken—probably because of the hideous practices of factory farming. Cuts of meat may be sometimes surprising, and the variety of things from the sea that are considered edible is downright amazing.

Wine and beer, of course, are two of the best reasons for exploring Europe. As for alternative beverages, tap water is perfectly safe in most places, as we have said, but you may want to explore the wide variety of interesting bottled mineral waters. The ubiquitous soft drink in Europe is not cola but Fanta, which comes in several fruit flavors.

SHOP PATTERNS

The nature of small shops varies surprisingly from country to country, and getting the hang of this is one of the most important keys to shopping skillfully in Europe. To illustrate: at home (with regional variations) we have the supermarket, the bakery, the delicatessen, the minimarket, and the liquor store. Without thinking about it, you know that the salami is probably best at the delicatessen, the liquor store stays open late, the supermarket is probably open on Sunday but the bakery probably isn't, and the liquor store will also sell milk. Each type of store overlaps some with the others, but each has its own specialties. These expectations are something you would never think of explaining to a foreign visitor, because you just *know* them. Every country in Europe has its own such pattern, and absorbing it takes a while in a new place.

One of the things we've tried to do in the country-by-country list that follows is to give you a head start about this. Other things we've tried to cover are the particularly good buys in each country, and national variations on closing hours. We have also made a few suggestions for eating in restaurants that are distinctive but won't use up a week's travel money. And for each country we have given you a menu or two, along with our happy memories of the circumstances.

COUNTRY-BY-COUNTRY FOOD SHOPPING GUIDE

BRITAIN

Perhaps your plane has landed in London and you're starting out by exploring the British Isles for awhile. If so, you'll have an easy time making the transition to shopping abroad because, obviously, there is no language problem, and all Americans who have read Pooh, Mary Poppins, and Ian Fleming have an instinctive feel and even a faint nostalgia for British shops. Don't be put off by the deplorable reputation of English food. There are excellent raw materials to be found, and what you do with them in your van kitchen is not going to be English cooking even if you are in England (or Scotland or Ireland or Wales).

Shop Patterns

There's the butcher, the baker, the greengrocer where you buy vegetables, and the fruiterer where you buy fruit, and of course you've heard of the tobacconist and the chemist and the ironmonger (getting a nice cozy glow, are you?).

What to Buy

The general rule for eating well in England is to keep it simple and natural. The rainy British climate is very good for vegetables. In residential neighborhoods you'll find lots of small shops, often run by Pakistanis, with lovely produce displayed in slanted boxes on the sidewalk and a few groceries inside. In early summer try the tender young peas or the little strawberries and raspberries. To eat with the latter, a costly but worth-every-penny delight is Devonshire clotted cream, or "double cream."

English roast beef is famous, but of course you can't do a whole joint on a van stove. Try some nice thick lamb chops instead (but make sure they're not mutton unless you like its stronger flavor). English cheese is honest and plain, but sometimes excellent. Look for Cheddar, Stilton, Cheshire, and Wensleydale. The best bread is a large, formidable wheaty entity with a stiff crust, from which you saw two slices to go with your cuppa.

Tea is a national institution, and you'll want to explore several different varieties and perhaps tuck some away for gifts. Beer in the British Isles is a complex subject, ranging from sweet dark stout to light clear bitter and all the gradations in between. They never refrigerate it and, believe it or not, you'll come to appreciate the fuller flavor it has when served at cellar temperature.

We have a fondness for the heavy, high-carbohydrate things like sausage rolls and scones that are sold in English bake shops to be eaten at tea, but you'll have to make up your own mind about them. In the interests of research you might even want to try a Chocolate Digestive, a sort of round graham cracker coated with imitation chocolate.

If you like curry, stash away a couple of boxes of Bolst's—one to use on your trip and one to take home. It's hard to find on the Continent. Ditto mango chutney, and other Indian condiments.

Closing Hours

Shops generally close at five or so, but snack shops can be open until ten or eleven. There is lunch hour closing in the villages, but not in London. Everything is shut on Sunday. Pub hours are eleven a.m. to eleven p.m., and noon to three p.m. and seven to ten-thirty p.m. on Sunday, although occasionally in the villages you may encounter places that observe the old custom of closing in the afternoon from two-thirty to five p.m.

Eating Out

We used to say that you haven't been to the British Isles unless you've eaten fish and chips hot out of a newspaper. But alas, with the incursion of more Continental ideas about food and more sophisticated ideas about cholesterol, and with the invasion of fast-food joints run by Chinese, Indian, and American franchise holders, fish and chips shops are dying out. Even when you do find one, some spoil-sport magistrate has ruled that wrapping the hot fish in newspaper is unsanitary. Is nothing sacred?

A traditional meal you *can* find, and one worth seeking out, is high tea or cream tea. Although you can put together the food quite handily in the van (see menu on next page), the ambience of pretty china, flowers, and dark rafters should be experienced in a tea shop at least once. Served at four o'clock, it makes dinner out of the question, but so what.

The best reasonably priced restaurant food in London is Indian, and if you're staying at the Crystal Palace campground, do not miss the superb Eastern Paradise tandoori restaurant at 36 Westow Hill, within easy walking distance.

Menus
Dinner by the Grace of Her Majesty the Queen

We were enjoying this supper amidst the Queen's roses in Regent's Park (where we had been living for two weeks) when the bobby finally knocked us up (on the window) and suggested with exquisite politeness that it would be appreciated if we would leave after dessert. He was so nice it didn't even spoil our dinner.

- Warm ale
- Small tomatoes to be eaten out of hand
- Thick lamb chops
- New peas and tiny onions
- Wholemeal (whole wheat) bread and butter
- Fresh raspberries and assorted tea biscuits
- Hot tea

Cream Tea at Stonehenge

After a day when we had our protein and veggies at noon, we decided to indulge ourselves with this traditional tea while we watched the setting sun bless the mysterious ancient stones with rose-colored light.

- Cucumber and watercress sandwiches on buttered brown bread (quartered, crusts removed, and pressed flat)
- Currant scones
- Cream buns with raspberry jam inside
- Strawberries with clotted cream
- Lots of hot tea

FRANCE
(and Belgium and French-speaking Switzerland)

All gourmet roads lead to Gaul and Lyon is Mecca, to thoroughly mix a geographical metaphor. The French have a national obsession with good food and you can reap the exquisite results of that divine madness. The real problem when shopping in France is to exercise enough self-restraint to keep dinner down to a mere feast rather than a culinary orgy. Plan to spend a bit more on food in France. You could eat more simply for less, but good heavens, why?

We don't pretend that what we do in our van in France is French cooking. That is art, and takes far more equipment and skill than we have at our command. No, we humbly admit that what we are eating so happily is California cooking with French groceries.

As a matter of fact, you can be extremely well fed without ever lighting the stove, except for after-dinner coffee. An American schoolteacher couple on a long RV summer explained it all to us. "What you do in France," she said happily, "is you go to the charcuterie and you buy all this stuff, and then..." (and her husband nodded eagerly) "you take it back to the van and you *eat* it!"

Shop Patterns

You think America is the home of the supermarket? You'll change your mind on your first visit to a French hypermarche. Cap 3000 near Cannes is a prime example. Imagine, first, half a mile of food under one roof. Shelves and shelves and shelves of real stuff, not cleaning supplies or cosmetics or convenience pseudo-food. Six kinds of canned mushrooms. A whole refrigerator case of nothing but caviar. Another for fresh pasta. A long, long counter of whole freshly caught fish of infinite variety with a corps of butchers standing by to fillet or butterfly to your specifications. Dozens of big wicker baskets of shellfish—shrimp, crab, and winkels and cockels and mussels and male and female sea urchins. . . Cheeses! Brie and camembert and roquefort and hundreds

Food Shopping

French hypermarches are enormous. (Photo by David Shore)

of others, stacked in big wheels to be cut to your wishes, or shrink-wrapped and labeled in a long case. . .

Wine! Rows and rows of dark gleaming bottles from every region of France, to every purse. A stand-up coffee bar where you can pause to get control of your reeling senses, and consult with the pleasant white-coated specialist who will offer you several tiny cups of various brews to sample and then grind a half kilo of your choice. Then on to the meat counters where butchers kind and dignified as brain surgeons preside over tender entre-cotes and escallopes de veau and also dressed larks, wild hare, boned and rolled canard... An alcove devoted entirely to sausages and sauerkraut. A gigantic charcu-terie like an art gallery with everything from tiny lobster tails in aspic to stuffed grape leaves. And we haven't even mentioned the pates or the pastry counters like an anorexic's nightmare, with fantasies in chocolate and meringue and whipped cream.

Naturally you can spend a fortune in one of these hypermarches, but you can also spend a moderate amount, have a wonderful time doing it, and come out with better than moderate groceries. (Last year we spent from $12 to $20 a day to eat in France, for the two of us.)

There are a number of nationwide chains of these megamarkets, usually with names that denote bigness: Mammoth, Hippo, Geant Casino, Auchan. (Most of these chains have recently branched out into Spain, Italy, and even the Netherlands.) They are usually on the outskirts of towns since they need so much land, and often their huge signs and vast parking lots can be spotted from the highway. Or you can find one by driving around in any town; you'll soon see billboards or signs painted on walls with arrows directing you through a maze of streets to the Auchan or the Hippo.

In descending order of size, the next kind of French food shop is the smaller neighborhood supermarket. These have less lavish selections, but are very good, nonetheless. Names to watch for are Prisunic or Monoprix. In Switzerland look for the Migros or the Co-op. The hypermarche companies, too, have smaller versions.

In spite of all this bounty at the supermarket, the French housewife also likes to go out in the morning with her basket on her arm and buy fresh for that day from small shops where she can discuss quality and price with the owner. At least a third of the businesses on any street will be food stores of some sort. There is the boulangerie for bread and croissants, the patisserie for pastry, the cave for wine, the fromagerie for cheese and butter, the poissonerie for fish, the charcuterie for assorted deli, and the boucherie for meat. (But beware of the butcher shop called chevaline—the brass stallion's head posted outside will tell you what's in the display case.)

Weekly open-air markets are everywhere, even in the streets of Paris and the posh resorts of the Riviera. Neighborhood stores, too, often have excellent produce, but supermarkets tend to be deficient in this area.

What to Buy

The endless variety can be confusing, but you really can't go too far wrong no matter what you buy. An experience not to be overlooked are haricots verts, tiny sliver-thin green beans. Cheeses are a whole subject in themselves. Stores divide them into firm cheeses like Camembert and soft spreadable cream cheeses like neufchatel. An exquisite but little-known type is marcelline, a grainy white semi-soft round wrapped in pear leaves—look for the brand name "Banon." In Normandy "brie" means "cheese" and you can have the clerk cut you a great big wedge for fifty cents.

Wonderful wines, too (it almost goes without saying), can be had for as little as 12 francs a bottle, although it probably is a better idea to pay a bit more—say 25 or 30 francs. You *can* spend a great deal more if your palate is sophisticated enough to make it worthwhile. Look at the label to make sure it's "sec," or dry; "demi-sec" is usually too sweet for American taste. Look also for the words "appelation controlee," your guarantee that the wine inside is a genuine product of the region indicated.

"The memory of a good French pate can haunt you for years," says Julia Child, and right she is. The experience—smooth and light, subtly spiced, embedded with surprises of bits of mushroom or lean ham or veal—is one that is rare for most Americans. You can buy pate in cunning little jugs or terrines or even in glass jars and cans, but by far the best way is to ask for a slice from the freshly-made bowls you'll see displayed at the charcuterie. A little goes a long way because it is so rich, and a nice piece of pate with a salad and bread makes a pleasant lunch or light supper.

Bread is important in France, and no wonder, because as everyone agrees, French bread is the definitive good bread. You'll find it at the boulangerie or sometimes the patisserie. There are several sizes and shapes, all with their own names, ranging from the thin crisp baguette through the wider batard all the way up to the big loaf called pain de compagne, which can weigh as much as two kilos. Prices are posted, and very cheap. Naturally you'll want to pick up croissants for breakfast. Buy fresh for every meal because the one defect of French bread is that it goes stale in a few hours. (Ducks and swans in public parks think this is an excellent quality because they are the final recipients of yesterday's staff of life.) In the early morning and late afternoon all the cyclists and strollers will have a long loaf tucked in a bag or basket or under their arms. With your own crisp baguette in hand you'll feel a pleasant sense of belonging.

In French-speaking Switzerland the food patterns are similar, with the addition of superb dairy products and the best chocolate in the world. Lindt, Suchard and Tobler are the most famous. Don't miss the dark chocolate bars filled with liquid cognac or kirsch.

Closing Hours

The two-hour lunch (le midi) is sacred. If your stomach can take it, you might try arranging your schedule to accomodate the main meal at noon.

Evening closing is at five or five-thirty, and one o'clock on Saturday. Most small shops in the countryside are often closed on Monday. Your daily baguette is the one food item you can buy on Sunday or Monday; on each block there will be one shop open for bread-buyers.

Eating Out

Who are we to tell you that on which Michelin and scores of others have built publishing empires? Of course you'll want the experience of a French meal in a restaurant, but expect to pay dearly unless you've been very selective. Dress as well as you can—Parisian waiters are not above ignoring you completely if your appearance doesn't come up to their standards. A book that we have found invaluable is *Cheap Eats in Paris* by Sandra A. Gustafson (Chronicle Books). Gourmet friends recommend Patricia Wells' *A Food Lover's Guide to France* (Workman Press) and the red Michelin guide for their advice on eating well in both Paris and the rest of the country. In the provinces you'll want to seek out little cafes that serve the local specialties at non-tourist prices—crepes in Brittany, for instance, or bouillabaise near Marseille, or choucroute in Alsace. A very welcome option both in Paris and the countryside is the motel-restaurant chain Chez Campanile, which serves bountiful French country cooking for astonishingly low prices.

Menus
Parisian Picnic for a Hot Night

One sultry August evening in the Bois de Vincennes when Paris sizzled we took a light supper down to a bench at the edge of the lake. Strollers wished us "Bon appetit!" as they looked to see what was on the menu. As the dusk deepened a group of West African students in native garb ambled past, harmonizing quietly with a guitar as they walked. Their cigarettes were winking red points in the dark, and on the lake swans were white smudges against the water. Later that night the suffocating heat broke with a storm, and big warm drops pelted down on our skylight. We and all the other vanners who were camped in the park slammed open our doors and ran exulting on the wet grass.

- Chilled (in the lake) Alsatian Sylvaner
- Thick slices of big beefsteak tomatoes
- Mushrooms, minced onion, and green olives in oil and lemon
- Pate d'poivre verte (a piquant pate with hot green peppers)
- Crisp baguette with butter
- Fresh peaches
- Coffee

Cap 3000 Pig-Out

After an orgiastic shopping spree at the monster supermarket, Cap 3000, we found a lovely camping spot on the maroon cliffs of the Corniche d'Or and watched the sunset and the turquoise blue waves below while we happily stuffed ourselves.

- Sparkling rose *and* rose d'Anjou.
- A whole jar of black caviar (oeuf du lompe, actually) with bread and sweet butter
- Tiny red and white radishes
- Pate ardennaise (a pate with big chunks of ham)
- Escalope de veau (veal scallops) sauteed in butter with small whole mushrooms, chopped parsley, and a splash of red wine

- Haricots verts briefly simmered in chicken broth
- A meltingly ripe Camembert
- Big purple plums
- Chocolate-filled chocolate eclairs
- Coffee

Liver in Lausanne

Liver and onions is a homely dish, but an entirely different thing when the slices of delicate veal liver are fresh cut by the butcher to your specifications of ultra thinness and then perfectly trimmed, when the onions are tiny shallots, and the dish is cooked quickly to perfect crisp pinkness in a generous dollop of new sweet butter. We assembled this dinner one golden hazy afternoon in Lausanne, Switzerland, when we had been climbing the steep cobbled streets and exploring the medieval part of town. We came back to our van by Lake Geneva with our arms loaded with packages, and after dinner we took our coffee out on the quay to watch the moon rise.

- Blanc de blancs
- St. Paulin (a firm white cheese)
- Foie de veau sauteed with shallots
- Zucchini and tomatoes topped with browned garlic bits
- Soup from the vegetable broth
- Chambord cassis (black currant pudding with whipped cream, in a little plastic cup, from the dairy case)
- Coffee

GERMANY
(and Austria and German-speaking Switzerland)

German food seems to the traveler to center around wurst. You'll see it in shop windows in loops and

strings and bunches and piles and you'll smell its glorious garlicky fragrance from street vendors and
Schnellimbissen (fast-food shops) everywhere. This is
an oversimplified picture of the national cuisine, but
since the heavy, luscious German home cooking involves
long baking or simmering and so is out of the question
for a van kitchen, when you cross the border into a
German-speaking country for all van purposes you are
in the Land of Wurst and Beer. Rejoice.

Shop Patterns

You won't find huge supermarkets here. Look for
more modest establishments labeled "Lebensmittel" or
"Grosshandel." Chains are Deutsche Supermarkt, Spar,
Plus, Penny Markt, Neckermanns, Co-op. Two discount
outlets with limited stock but spectacular savings are
Norma and Aldi. Some of the best grocery stores are
hidden away in the basements of department stores—
check the C & A or the Kaufhaus in almost any city or
town. The gourmet lower floor of the big Munich
Kaufhof in the Marienplatz is spectacular, reasonably
priced, centrally located for post-sightseeing shopping,
and has a wonderful deli counter of prepared salads and
cooked meats. The Viktualienmarkt, also near the
Marienplatz in Munich, is one of the most interesting
outdoor markets in Europe.

Mom-and-pop groceries are plentiful in smaller
towns but there are also specialty shops: the Backerei
for bread and rolls, the Obst und Gemuse store for fruit
and vegetables, and—most important—the Metzgerei,
or butcher. Meat-cutting and wurst-stuffing is a valued
profession here. In Northern Germany you may see
gruesome displays of dead flesh artistically arranged in
butcher shop windows: pyramids and mounds of roasts

and chops festooned by serpentine whirls of sausage links and graced with little china pigs and cows.

WHAT TO BUY

Well, wurst, of course. Any respectable butcher shop will carry at least a dozen kinds, both fresh and smoked. Salami is superb, and comes in four or five varieties. Liverwurst or braunschweiger is also vastly better than anything you've ever called by those names. Try, too, bratwurst, mettwurst, knackwurst, jagdwurst, and all the others. We usually just point to something that looks good; at first we tried to associate names with varieties, but then we noticed that there seemed to be very little consistency about wurst nomenclature from region to region. In Bavaria sample the weisswurst, a white sausage made from veal and parsley. Wurst is an ideal van food—it can be fried or grilled or steamed in a trice; it can be sliced hot in vegetables or soup or omelets or cold in salads and sandwiches, and the smoked kinds keep for days without refrigeration. An indispensable accompaniment is a sharp mustard, or "senf," but it's not for sissies.

Other meats, particularly pork and ham, are also very good and moderately priced. We recommend the thick pork chops or the Kassler Rippiert, a smoked ham-like chop that is excellent cold with German potato salad (which you can also buy at the butcher shop). The names of meat cuts in German can be a minor culture shock: "Schwein," for instance, for "pork," or "gehackte Fleisch," which sounds hideously like "hacked flesh" but is really only hamburger.

German bread is grim—hard and dark and solid—but not without its own charm. We came to call it affectionately "rockbread." Kaiser rolls are standard for breakfast and they can be found even when other fresh bread is scarce. An amazingly tough and probably very healthy food is Vollkornbrot (whole grain bread). This square dense loaf is made of several kinds of whole grain, and it lasts forever. Sliced very thin with butter or cheese, it's quite tasty in a chewy sort of way. Once when crossing the Continent on a long journey we bought some Vollkornbrot and used a few slices, and then forgot about it. The passing kilometers vibrated it to the back of the cupboard and then down into a hidden crevice. Seven weeks later when we were enduring the scarcities of southern Yugoslavia, a thorough rummage in the larder uncovered our long-lost loaf, as good as new, and we ate it happily.

A Bavarian specialty that is very adaptable for van cooking are the delicious egg noodles called spatzle. Try them with a simple sauce of butter and garlic, or cooked in chicken broth with a handful of shredded cheese stirred in at the last. German cheese is not famous, but happily French and Dutch types are readily available. In German Switzerland Emmantaler is our old friend "Swiss cheese" but minus most of the holes.

Interesting produce buys are huge white radishes to be sliced paper thin and eaten with beer, wild brown forest mushrooms, which you'll see in Munich at street stands in early fall, and glorious big white grapes from the Rhine and Mosel Valleys.

A brand of chocolate called Rittersport is ubiquitous, very good, and comes in some surprising flavors.

German wine is a revelation. Evidently the best vintages are too fragile to be exported, or maybe the Germans just want to drink it all at home. In any case, you'll be delighted with their flowery, spicy delicacy. An itinerant street musician with more taste than cash taught us how to buy. "Never spend more than four marks," he proclaimed, and we've never failed to find an exquisite wine at that price.

At first we made earnest attempts to record and memorize the five-syllable, two-word names of each wonderful bottle, but then we learned that vintages change not only their quality but their character from year to year, so such efforts are pointless. Now we look only for the words "Qualitatswein" (quality wine) or "Qualitatswein mit pradikat" (quality wine with special features).

Beer is a staple. Lowenbrau, you probably know, has its home in Munich, and you'll recognize other brands, too. When in Bavaria try Weissbier, a beer made from wheat, served with a slice of lemon floating on top.

CLOSING HOURS

Doors shut at the usual five-thirty, and promptly at two on Saturday. Sunday is the day of rest and no shopping. Every fourth Saturday is "lange Samstag," when shops stay open until six.

EATING OUT

Since you can't do real German cooking in the van, you'll have to seek it out in a restaurant, unless you make friends who invite you home for dinner. Look for authentic places where the architecture is like an arched cave with stylized birds and flowers painted on the walls. Zur Bratzen, 72 Leopoldstrasse in the Schwabing aea of Munich is a prime example. You might order the Schweinbraten (roast pork) with Blaukraut (sweet and sour red cabbage) and semmelknodeln (tiny dumplings), and afterward if you have room (which isn't likely) share a piece of dampf nudeln (literally translated "wet noodles"—

but it isn't. Traditionally eaten on washday as the entire meal, this million-calorie treat is a rich sponge cake doused with custard sauce.). You'll also not want to miss the quintessential German experience of the beer garden.

Menus
Snug Bavarian Supper for a Cold Rainy Night

Since it's often more or less raining in Germany, you'll need to cook something substantial and comforting on chilly evenings. On our first visit to Munich we lived behind the grim forbidding stone pile of the Deutsches Museum, and on dark moonless nights we needed all the comfort we could get to ward off the stony stares of the centaurs and griffins and other looming mythological statues on the parapets.

- Lowenbrau beer
- Thin slices of white radish and purple onion with a squeeze of lemon and a sprinkle of salt
- Individual loaves of Zwiebelbrot (onion bread)
- Bratwurst fried with onions and potatoes
- Rittersport yogurt-chocolate bar
- Lots of coffee with milk

Alpine Serenity

The picturesque mountain villages of the Bavarian Alps can be jammed with tourists in July and August. We were lucky. We found an abandoned hotel with a deserted parking lot high on the side of a mountain. There we snuggled our van in under a pine tree where we had a view of rolling green meadows and forest. At sunset, after a long hike, we enjoyed a savory stew to the accompaniment of distant cowbells as a farmer and his dog across the valley herded the cattle home for evening milking.

- Rudesheimer Rosengarten (a flowery white wine)
- Green pepper strips
- Emmantaler cheese slices
- Schweinschnitzel stew (sliced pork tenderloin, browned with vegetables and simmered in lentil soup from a mix)
- Kaiser rolls
- Coffee
- Big white grapes

GREECE

When you're traveling in the glorious land of Hellas, it simply doesn't pay to try to cook in the van. The tavernas are charming and the food you will find there is universally delicious and astonishingly cheap. Conversely, grocery shopping is difficult, time-consuming, and not especially economical. You may want, however, to lay in supplies for breakfasts and for one emergency meal in case you find yourself at nightfall in a beautiful but remote sleepsite, and you will certainly want to have some picnics in this land that offers the most beautiful outdoors in all Europe.

Shop patterns

The word for grocery store is (phonetically) "pahn-do-po-*lee*-o" but recognizing it in the Greek alphabet is a day's work. Luckily, even the tiniest little hole-in-the-wall will have a big proud sign that proclaims "Super Market." Here you can buy everything except bread. Because of the heat and the price of electricity, small groceries often do not turn on the lights in the daytime, so you must peer around in the dim recesses to find what you want. It makes sense to carry a flashlight when shopping.

Bakeries sell only bread. The loaves are shoveled hot out of the big oven and are snatched up before they cool by eager customers, so buy yours early in the day or there may be none left. There are two kinds; the braided loaf is sweet. For pastries, find a coffee cafe or an ice cream bar and look for the display counter in the back. There are also stores that specialize in fruits and vegetables

Butcher shops are appalling to American sensibilities: a shop open to the street where carcasses are hung in full view and the butcher presides over a wooden block in a bloody apron, wielding a cleaver in one hand and a fly swatter in the other. We confine our meat purchases to salami, but that doesn't stop us from enjoying the wonderful souvlaki and baby lamb chops in the tavernas.

In Greece you will not find the open markets that are so much a part of the food supply pattern in other parts of Europe. The closest equivalent is the market section of large cities.

What to Buy

For your picnic, you'll want a big hunk of feta—a white, crumbly salty cheese made from goat or sheep's milk. Every store has it, but they keep it in a can under the counter. Ask, and the proprietor will dip you out a chunk of the size you gestured. When you store it, be sure to wrap it in double layers of plastic—it leaks.

Olives must also be requested. They are saltier, softer, and much more delicious than the California variety, and they range from tiny black wrinkled things to great glossy green beauties. Except in large cities, what you get is what you get, because any particular store will have only one kind. Never mind, they're all good.

The Greeks make some pleasant wines for tourists, but once you get used to the resinous tang of retsina you'll find it the perfect accompaniment to Greek food. And cheap; a half bottle costs less than a dollar. But the first time you taste it, you'll think they're kidding.

Ouzo, too, is a national institution. Every town has several ouzerias, cafes where men while away the evening (and the afternoon) playing backgammon and sipping this fiery licorice-flavored brandy. Put away a bottle in the van for medicinal and other purposes.

Although all the pastries are good, a special Greek delight is baklava, layers of tissue-thin crust or shredded wheat filled with honey and ground nuts. With it, drink a cup of Greek coffee (which you must never refer to as "Turkish coffee") and then drink a glass of water.

In grocery stores, coffee comes in two varieties: the fine powder for Greek style, and "Nes" (Nescafe). If you want anything else, bring it with you.

Closing Hours

The afternoons in this hot country are devoted to sleeping or sitting quietly in the shade playing backgammon. Even the dogs sleep heavily in the street. If you miss the morning shopping hours, wait until the sun goes down for another chance. Sunday closing is not quite so rigorously observed as in other places.

Eating Out

The tavernas are one of the best parts of traveling in Greece. These are little outdoor restaurants with wobbly tables covered in oilcloth and mismatched chairs. Always there are flowers and vines growing up poles overhead and bouzouki music. They all have wonderful food, even the most humble, and they all are very clean and incredibly cheap. You have to wait around until a decent Greek hour for dinner—say, eight o'clock. Then you go in, pick out a table with a good view of the sea or the sidewalk parade or the band, and when the waiter comes you all traipse back into the kitchen to see what's on the menu. They open the oven and uncover the pots to show you the cooked dishes like moussaka and stuffed peppers, and then they even display the raw meat for grilled chops or shish kebab and pull out drawers of fish. You point to your choice and then go back to your table and pretty soon the waiter's assistant comes bustling out with a nice clean sheet of paper or plastic, which he lays over the table and fastens at the corners with a rubber band or clothespin in case of wind.

Then the waiter himself brings the wine. If it's retsina, he plunks down the tumblers, and with a flourish he flips off the cap with a bottle-opener as if he were drawing the cork on the finest champagne. Then comes a basket with the napkins, forks and knives and bread (no butter—don't ask for it), and at last the food. Always there is a Greek salad—a big dish of tomatoes and cucumbers and olives with rings of purple onions and a big slice of feta on top. (One order is enough for two) For a change, try tzatziki, yogurt with shredded cucumbers and garlic. Lamb is delicious, as is the fresh-caught grilled fish, especially the tiny crisp red mullet. Outside of Athens the check will almost never be more than seven dollars total. A tip is insulting, and if you fall into conversation with the owner as you're leaving he will most likely offer you a glass of ouzo on the house. For coffee and dessert, wander down the street and find a lively cafe (but not an ouzeria unless you're an all-male party). After that, on to the outdoor disco, where you can dance away the night like Zorba.

Menus
 Aegean Idyll

This seems to us to be the classic Greek picnic. We ate it on an exquisite stretch of isolated beach, where we settled down on the golden sand with our backs against a sun-warmed rock and our toes in the pale turquoise water. Afterwards a long nap in the sun and a swim.

- Feta cheese
- Hunks of fresh-baked bread
- A huge tomato
- Olives
- Slivers of onion
- A swig of ouzo to clear the palate
- Pale green figs we picked from a tree beside the path to the beach

ITALY

Italy, while a driver's nightmare, is a van cook's paradise. The produce is perfection: gigantic yellow and red and green peppers, and tomatoes so beautiful you want to photograph them before you slice, fresh basil, tiny tender zucchini . . . The coffee is the best in the world, and if you're caffeine nuts like we are you'll have trouble not blowing your whole food budget on endless cups of espresso and cappuccino. And pasta is an excellent raw material for van meals.

Shop Patterns

There is only one drawback to shopping in Italy, but unfortunately it can be a serious annoyance. Italians, for some reason probably related to the extended family, often assume you are buying food for at least eight people. At the supermarket everything comes in gigantic packages. Therefore your best bet may be to look for small neighborhood groceries where they will accommodate your meager needs and where the shop people are unfailingly patient and gracious. Most often these little stores sell a bit of everything, and the sign will say "alimentari" (groceries) or "fruta e verdura" (fruits and vegetables). The pasticceria sells pastry but very little bread (oddly enough, bread is often hard to find). The macelleria has meat, and also cheese, butter, salami, eggs, and some pasta and sauces.

What to Buy

Because you probably don't have a great big pot for spaghetti or linguini, give preference to pasta in small shapes like shells and bows and wheels. Sauces come in little glass jars in a bewildering variety. One is enough because they are so flavorful that you don't need to drown the pasta. Tortellini is nice, and a real treasure is chicken or beef or cheese ravioli, fresh-made and displayed with pride on the top of the butcher case. It's so good in its own right that it's a pity to muffle the flavor with tomato sauce. Try simmering it for just a few minutes in chicken broth or bouillon.

Another fine Italian invention is gnocchi, tiny potato and flour dumplings. When married with a smooth, creamy sauce of rich gorgonzola cheese, they are one of the world's great dishes. Italian cold cuts are excellent, as are gorgonzola, mozzarella, and other cheeses. But the real glory, the reason we are always reluctant to leave Italy and go eat somewhere else, is the true Parmesan, known there as "Parmigiano-Reggiano." It looks terrible: big ugly misshapen chunks of a pale dried-out substance like gum eraser. Buy some. Grate it on anything you're cooking. Instant ambrosia!

In the unlikely event that you should get tired of pasta, veal is superb in Northern Italy. Since the flavor needs a bit of help from wine and sauces, experiment a bit, or ask a housewife at the butcher's counter for advice. Even across language barriers Italians love to give cooking instruction, and you may find, as I did, that you've started an emotional discussion between two ladies with conflicting convictions about how long to simmer the ravioli.

Italian wines are cheap and generally excellent, with a distinctive character. Experiment beyond chianti with the rich rough reds, the strong assertive whites. Spumanti is bubbly and a bit sweet, but nice for after dinner on a warm evening.

Closing Hours

Food shops close at noon, and don't reopen until three, or four, or five—or not at all on Wednesday afternoon. The usual early Saturday and all day Sunday closings apply.

Eating Out

Forget pizza. Like chop suey, some people maintain, it's an American invention that has bounced back to the mother country. Instead, seek out the subtle veal and seafood dishes of the north and explore the wide variety of pastas beyond spaghetti and ravioli.

Menus
Anticipating the Grand Prix

The night before the big auto race we settled into the city park of Monza, surrounded by hundreds of happy Italian vanners and tenters. While they waved banners of Ferrari red, we ate a green dinner.

- D'Aquino Soave (a dry white wine)
- Roasted peppers in olive oil with green olives (turn the peppers on the open flame until the skin is black, then peel and seed them)
- Fusilli with pesto (sauce from a jar)
- Breadsticks and butter
- Green grapes and Bel Paese cheese
- Coffee

View of Firenze

While Florence is an art lover's paradise, it's hell to drive in. We were relieved to be in the campground across the river on the hilltop, where we could admire its rooftops from a picturesque distance and enjoy a restoring feast.

- Bellosguarda Bianca di Toscana
- Sliced red and yellow and green peppers, tiny radishes, dressed with lemon and salt
- Gnocchi con gorgonzola (boil the gnocchi gently for about seven minutes, then drain well and stir in a generous amount of small pieces of the cheese)
- Long green beans
- Crusty rolls and sweet butter
- Chocolate pastries
- Coffee

THE NETHERLANDS

For geographic reasons the Netherlands may be the first country you visit on the Continent. Happily, it is an excellent place in which to practice your shopping skills because nearly everyone under fifty speaks English and because the Dutch are extraordinarily nice to foreigners. The food is plain and hearty but clean and fresh. And there is the exotic bonus of Indonesian cuisine.

Shop Patterns

"Cozy" is the definitive word in Holland and you will find that it applies to the food shops as well as the bars and cafes. There are good supermarkets outside Amsterdam, although in the city you will be more likely to find small grocery stores. You can recognize them even from the end of the block by the display of produce set out on the sidewalk in wooden boxes.

Every town has a weekly open-air market, some of them quite picturesque. The famous cheese market in Alkmaar is a good one. Check with the tourist bureau (the VVV) opposite the Central Station in Amsterdam for a list of days and times.

The "warme bakker" shop will have a good selection of still-warm bread, cookies, and heavy crumbly tarts. Butcher shops come in several kinds. The generic term is "slagerij" but some of them specialize in "vlees" (red meat), "kip" or "polterei" (chicken), or cold cuts and cheese. There are shops that concentrate on cheese, and these will also carry excellent butter and eggs, and sometimes milk and yogurt. Some butcher shops are for Moslems and carry only ritually slaughtered lamb and beef. You'll recognize these by the Arabic groceries stacked in the window.

Fish stores abound. The sign will say "vis" or "vis-handel." Inside you will find fresh and smoked fillets, small whole fried fish, either hot or cold, and tiny raw herring fillets (holl haring) meant to be eaten raw with onions. (This Dutch treat is also sold from vending stands in the streets on nice summer days. The traditional modus operandi is to hold the fish up by the tail, throw back your head, and devour it in three brave bites. The onions help.)

The "snackbar" is a peculiarly Dutch institution, and

fills the social function of the American neighborhood liquor store, taco stand, candy store, hamburger joint, and videogame arcade. They are often local hangouts, especially for teenagers, and a fine place to get something to eat when you're in a hurry, haven't got much money, or everything else is closed. They also make the best French fries ("patats") in the entire universe. You can have them with a squirt of mayonnaise or curry or sate (an Indonesian peanut sauce), but not with catsup. Other things on the menu are "krokettes" (spicy ground meats on a stick deep-fried to order), broodjes (small soft buttered buns filled with ham or roast beef or cheese or shrimp or raw hamburger), and soft drinks and beer.

What to Buy

Growing things that like lots of rain love the Netherlands. We would especially recommend the tiny new potatoes, the baby carrots, the famous small Dutch tomatoes, and the edible-pod green peas.

Ham is definitely the meat of preference here. The butcher will slice it paper thin unless you tell him otherwise, but it's excellent that way and goes further. Don't be embarrassed to ask for just two or three slices; many Dutch people buy only enough for one sandwich at a time. Pork chops are also nice. A favorite of ours is Rotterdammer wurst—a long thin stick of spicy hard sausage like salami that is usually displayed as an impulse purchase on top of the butcher case.

Fish can be bought freshly cooked, either hot or cold, and makes an excellent (and very cheap) main dish for a van meal. The tiny holl haring are also very nice to saute lightly in butter.

In the warme bakker go for the lighter breads

because the dark whole wheat can be very heavy. Or try "fruit bread"—a slightly sweet loaf bejeweled with currants, raisins, citron, nuts and sometimes a tunnel filled with marzipan. Gingerbread is sold in a block and eaten for breakfast. It goes surprisingly well at that meal, and a loaf lasts a long time.

The Netherlands may be your only chance to buy peanut butter. Most Europeans are puzzled by our passion for the stuff, but the Dutch use it in Indonesian cooking and call it "pindar kaas."

Dutch chocolate is famous, and justly so. Verkade with hazelnuts is our favorite, but Tobler and Van Houten are excellent, too.

Dutch cheese is also highly esteemed. Edam and Gouda are the most famous, but don't miss Korsil (a smoky, firm smooth cheese with a brown rind) or Loidoe (a sharp dry cheese with caraway seeds). Cheese is categorized as "jong" (young) or "oud" (old); the oud may look dried out, but the flavor is mellower.

Beer in Holland means Heineken. The familiar green cans are everywhere, and it is not even too hard to find them cold. Amstel and Grolsch are excellent also.

Closing Hours

Shops close at five-thirty or six. Saturday closing is at two in the city, four in the suburbs or country. Everything is shut on Sunday, and some bakers and butchers stay closed on Monday. The snackbar is your salvation if you get caught short. Most stay open until ten, eleven, or even midnight and all day Sunday, and for van cooking they will sell you sliced ham or roast beef or cheese, plain broodjes (little sandwiches), butter, or a six-pack of cold beer.

Eating Out

The Indonesian restaurants of the Netherlands are not to be missed. They come in a range of prices and elegance, from the humble neighborhood cafe where you can have a plate of nasi goreng for 12 guilders, to the exotic and costly establishments near the Leidseplein, where you can recline in more-than-Oriental splendor and feast on a rijstafel of forty dishes, each spicier and more delicious than the last.

The unique Amsterdam vegetarian cafe called Egg Cream serves intricately spiced and hearty prix fixe meals in a funky atmosphere.

Menus
Canal Dinner

As we've explained above, in Holland you'll want to build your menus around the beautiful vegetables and the excellent hard cheeses and smoked fish. Here is a dinner we enjoyed while parked by a tranquil canal where barges and fishing boats and cabin cruisers chugged past. Invariably the crew would wave cheerfully from the deck as they glided by.

- Cold bottles of Heineken beer
- Salad of sweet red peppers, edible-pod peas, and tomatoes dressed with oil and lemon
- Chunks of hard caraway-flecked Oud Leidse cheese
- Braided bread with sweet butter
- Tiny herring fillets sauteed quickly in butter
- Fresh strawberries
- Coffee

Cozy Company Supper

Another day we made some new friends at the flea

market and invited everybody back to the van for dinner. It was chilly at the yacht harbor where we were staying, so the five of us squeezed into the front and back seats, and we started a soup to warm our hands and hearts. The preliminary courses were all more or less finger food, and the soup we shared out in cups and jelly glasses. Luckily we had four spoons. The two of *us* took turns. Afterwards we all sang each other our respective national folk songs.

- A shot of cranberry genever each for warmth (we passed the bottle to save dishwashing)
- Cold smoked and breaded fish (one per person) sprinkled with minced watercress and a squeeze of lemon
  - Heavily buttered brown bread topped with slices of brown-edged Korsil cheese
  - Cucumber and tomato wedges
  - Veal and noodle soup (from a mix) with tiny carrots, pearl onions, and thumb-sized new potatoes simmered in it
  - Gingerbread
  - Verkade milk chocolate bars with hazelnuts
  - Hot tea

PORTUGAL

Portugal has the delightful distinction, from the traveler's point of view, of being the last really cheap country in Western Europe. Because it is the most recent member of the Common Market, you will often see things still being done in the old way—people tilling the fields with teams of oxen or drawing water from a well with a treadmill. But this is no poverty-stricken culture. The Portuguese live simply but well, and they are unfailingly cheerful and relaxed. Every little town centers around a market hall where lovely fruits and flowers and vegetables and an astounding array of fresh seafood can be bought for pennies.

Shop Patterns

Although there are occasional supermarkets in larger towns, the best shopping is to be had at the above-mentioned market halls. However, these places are not easy to find. We usually look for a morning trail of people carrying plastic bags of food and follow their direction backward to the source, which will be a dark, sinister-looking warehouse sort of place. But step inside to a wonderland of stalls selling just-picked veggies, luscious fruits, eggs and cheeses. Go next door to another hall to find the seafood. (Presumably the fish hall is kept separate because it is hosed down every night to minimize the smell of the sea.) Bread, wine and beer, and other groceries can be bought at little shops that adjoin the market proper.

What to Buy

Obviously, fresh seafood is the thing here, and it is sold in eye-popping variety. In one typical market we saw three kinds of codfish, giant prawns, shrimp, crab, lobster, tiny clams, skate, squid of all sizes, eel, octopus, a gigantic swordfish, mussels, red bream, sardines, and a passel of other things with gills or shells that have no names that we know. The fisherpeople at the counters will slice a thick steak off a big fish or bone and fillet a small one, or even show you what to do with an octopus (but maybe you don't want to know).

Notable in the beautiful array of produce is the presence of sweet potatoes and broccoli (two vegetables almost never seen in other parts of Europe) and the gourmet delights of baby artichokes, Italian parsley, tiny new potatoes and peas, loquats, fava beans, and (in spring) gorgeous strawberries.

Other goodies to be had are little smoky black olives and local cheeses in small rounds. A surprise is the little box labeled Natas, which when shaken and opened yields a lovely thick cream that is heavenly spooned over peaches or strawberries. Bread is most often found in the form of hard round rolls that seem stale at first squeeze, but are actually quite moist and fresh inside. The ubiquitous presence of English tourists in Portugal has a benefit for other travelers: English bacon in the stores, which serves as a nice mini-ham for flavoring stir-fries as well as accompanying eggs for breakfast. Those flat white things you'll see stacked in boxes in every store are salted codfish, which the Portuguese use as a staple.

The national beer is Sagres, and it's just fine. Even better is the crisp, light white wine (vinho branco) and the sometimes sparkling but always interesting green wine (vinho verde). These often come in cute little squat round bottles that are difficult to throw away.

The first time we tried to find fresh milk in a Portuguese store we searched the place over three times, looking fruitlessly on the shelves where the clerks kept pointing. At last we found it—not in a bottle or a carton but a big plastic bag. The milk inside is okay, but pouring a glass of it from that floppy pillow (and worse, trying to find a way to set it down afterward) is a scene from Laurel and Hardy. After several tries we worked out a moderately successful technique: Hold the bag upright with both hands, get somebody else to nip off a small corner with scissors, and tip it into another container in one quick steady motion. And have a sponge ready for the inevitable spills.

Closing Hours

Like most warm southern European countries, Portugal regards afternoons as a time for sleeping. Markets are open until one, but then close for the day, or perhaps reopen briefly after three. Shop early.

Eating Out

Restaurants are simple and friendly and serve gigantic platters heaped with grilled fish or squid and fries. A useful phrase is "meia dose" which means "half portion." "Carne de porco a alentejana" (pork and clams in a coriander sauce) is nice, but watch out for "cozido a Portuguesa" (vegetable stew with intestines) or the perfectly awful boiled cod ("bacalao") with soggy potatoes and broccoli. Remember that on Monday here, as in all fishing countries, the seafood at restaurants will be Saturday's catch until at least late afternoon.

Menus
April in Portugal

One sunny spring day we drove the pretty little road that winds down to Sagres through hills white with wild roses, to the clifftop Fortaleza where Henry the Navigator's school trained explorers like Magellan and Vasco da Gama. After we had explored the ruins, we found a freecamp spot that looked out over the vast Atlantic and enjoyed this dinner, washed down with a beer named for that very spot.

- Sagres beer
- New peas stir-fried with English bacon and shallots
- Steamed and buttered sweet potatoes
- Crisp rolls
- Strawberries with natas
- Coffee

Homage to Olhao

Another day, a congenial but motley group of English-speaking campers (a South African family, an Australian family, a bicycling couple from Massachusetts with their twin sons, and us) spent a happy morning gathering our dinner at the Saturday market at Olhao, then piled onto the ferry to an offshore island for the day. Our Portuguese fellow passengers on the boat were in a holiday mood, laughing and singing and laden with their purchases: bags of vegetables and fish, a big yellow rosebush in a basket, even (on the lap of the man next to us) a young live chicken poking her head out of a shoebox tied with string. All day on the island we wandered through strange little sandy villages with tile-fronted houses and braved the stiff breezes on the wild beach. At sunset, after a few anxious moments, we saw the ferry coming to take us back to camp, where we all swam in the pool and then shared this good supper.

- Sparkling vinho verde
- Little smoky olives
- Giant prawns brushed with garlic butter and grilled on a friend's barbecue
- Steamed baby new potatoes and leafy broccoli
- Thick slices of peasant bread toasted on the grill
- Loquats and apricots
- Coffee

SCANDINAVIA
(Norway, Denmark, and Sweden)

Waiting to board the ferry that would take us to Norway, we met two young French university students who were heading north to study the wildlife. They were having lunch in their van from their bountiful cache of French groceries. "How's the food in Scandinavia?" we asked them (because the French always know about such things). "Terrible!" they cried, reaching for another bottle of Bordeaux. "Horrible! All plastic!" We put it down to chauvinism, but later we had to admit that it was a pretty accurate assessment. As Exhibit A, may we present frozen fish pudding cakes? Everything that can be preserved, canned, embalmed, shrink-wrapped, or frozen, is. And it's all very expensive. Luckily there are exceptions if you know how to spot them, and with a little luck and a few invitations to dinner, you can survive the culinary difficulties of the North.

Shop Patterns

As might be expected, food is sold mostly in supers. Look for Tempo in Sweden, Brugsen's in Denmark, and also check department store basements and gas stations. Open-air markets are once or twice a week in most towns. Co-op stores are common in Denmark, but they usually sell only in quantity.

What to Buy

Denmark (which is by far the best of the three, culinarily speaking) has some goodies: blue cheese, the exquisite chicken liver pate at Brugsen's deli in Copenhagen, Danish pastry (which is baked in a gigantic ring and sold by the yard), and very good beer. Famous brands are Carlsberg and Tuborg. They come in interesting varieties like red, green, and the super-strong elephant beer.

In Sweden concentrate on caviar (cheap) and the excellent slightly sweet breads and the rusk crackers. Milk is also very good here. Try filmjolk, a thick fermented milk product that is very nice with sliced fruit. The Swedes have made an art of exquisite cookies;

they're pricey but worth it.

In Norway, just try hard to make friends who will invite you home to eat and pray it doesn't turn out to be fish pudding cakes.

The most disappointing thing about food in Scandinavia is fish. We couldn't find any fresh to buy, no matter how often we pursued signs over stores that said "Fisk." All we ever found were repulsive reptilian things in jars, pickled like laboratory specimens. They do a lot of fishing, especially in Norway, and they can't turn it all over to the jar people, but where they sell it is a mystery. Norwegian friends tell us you have to go to the harbor very early in the morning, but pursuing this lead never got us anywhere.

Both Sweden and Norway have severe social problems with alcoholism, so beer and wine are taxed heavily. Consequently a glass of beer can easily cost five dollars in a cafe and almost that much from a shop (if you could even find it, that is). Bring your own from Denmark, but a word of caution: never, never drive after drinking in Scandinavian countries (or anywhere else, for that matter) because the law is extremely strict about this.

Eating Out

Sorry, we couldn't afford to research this for you, except for the elegant vegetarian buffet called Ortagarden, Nybrogatan 31, Stockholm. If price is no object, Danish open-face sandwiches and Swedish smorgasbord, of course, are the things to seek out.

Menu
Swedish Country Supper

Sweden is a huge sparsely populated country with farmlands—that look exactly like Minnesota, red barns and all—and dark pine forests bejeweled with lakes. This supper was eaten in a wooded glade late one evening after we had been boating under the midnight sun.

- Radishes and raw green peas eaten out of the pod
- Mandelbrod (a sweet braid) and butter
- Sodost (a sweet white cheese)
- Buttered carrots
- Blueberries and cherries
- An assortment of cookies: chocolate-covered marzipan fingers, rum balls, honeycake squares with chocolate frosting
- Lots of fresh milk

SPAIN

Ah, España! Here is one country that lives up to your fantasies. Because Spain was isolated from tourism for the years under Franco, it is less Americanized than the rest of Europe, and consequently some of it still looks just the way you imagined it would from teenage encounters with *Carmen* or *For Whom the Bell Tolls*. The food too is less standardized, and so you will have the opportunity for some new culinary experiences. Food in the tapa bars is so interesting and so cheap (occasionally even free) that you will want to eat there often while you are in towns.

Shop Patterns

Specialty stores are the panaderia (bread), pastilliceria (pastry), mantequilleria (cheese). Little grocery stores can be recognized by the sign that says "alimentacion" and by the curtain in the doorway, which is meant to keep out flies, not customers. The best place to shop for all kinds of food is in the central market ("mercado central"), which will be in a roofed plaza filled with booths. Look for more produce sellers out back.

What to Buy

Olive oil and garlic are the staples of Spanish cooking. Forget dairy products for a while and try the light, fragrant Spanish olive oil on your bread. If you ask for only one or two heads when you buy garlic, the farmer will shrug and throw it in free. What in the world could you want with such a minute quantity? he'll wonder. Olives, of course, are good, and near the coasts the seafood is plentiful and excellent (especially shrimp, mussels, and swordfish). The cheese to ask for is Mancheca.

The red wines of Spain from the Rioja region are as brisk and complex as a flamenco solo, and well worth sampling. Sherry, of course, is the glory of Spain, and comes in many moods, all mellow.

Closing Hours

You should visit the mercado in the morning, but otherwise Spain only really comes alive after dark in the summer, and many shops never open until the sun goes down and the people come out for the paseo, or evening walk. Siesta is sacred, and so is Sunday closing.

Eating Out

Every little bar in Spain displays a selection of tapas, or snacks, that you are expected to order with a drink. Ask for a cana (small glass of beer) or a fino (same of sherry) and point to what looks good. The waiter will give you a little dish of it, accompanied by bread, olives, and an extra fork for your friend. Later you can try something else, or move on to another bar for a new selection. The waiter will remember exactly how much you owe, and it will be very little (and don't tip).

Typical tapas are sliced ham or cheese, tortilla espanola (an egg and potato and onion omelet, usually served cold), champinones (mushrooms sauteed in garlic and olive oil), Russian salad, gambas a plancha (shrimp), calamari frita (crisp rings of French-fried squid). And many more. You eat standing up (if you sit down it looks touristy and costs more). When you want something more substantial you can ask for your tapa in a bocadillo (French roll) or order it in a large serving called a racion.

Menus
Spanish Swordfish Feast

We ate this beautiful meal in a pleasant shady campground on the Costa del Sol after driving all day through the brick-red plains and olive orchards of the interior.

- Smoky mancheca cheese
- Rioja wine
- Ratatouille of zucchini, tomatoes, onions, eggplant, and green beans with garlic and fresh dill
- Thick swordfish steaks, grilled with lemon slices
- Country bread and olive oil
- Cheremoya (a white custardy fruit) and persimmons
- Coffee

At Isaac El Sec

This one was such a perfect combination that we had to include it, even though we didn't cook it ourselves, but savored its pleasures in the beautiful patio of Isaac El Sec, a secret restaurant in the midst of the restored ruins of an ancient Cabalistic University in Girona.

- Melon draped with tissue-thin slices of prosciutto ham
- Basque chicken (fricaseed with green bell peppers, onions, and tomatoes)
- An icy pitcher of sangria
- A big basket of bread for sopping up the sauce
- Espresso

TURKEY

Mention Turkey to Americans and they'll shudder and mumble something about Midnight Express. But the horrors depicted in that movie were from another era. Nowadays the government in Turkey is eager to encourage tourism, and the Aegean and Mediterranean coasts in that country are the best travel bargain in Europe: safe, cheap, scenic, with comfortable accommodations and deliciously exotic sights everywhere. The Turks are overwhelmingly honest and friendly and genuinely pleased that you are visiting their land. Turkish food is one of the three great world cuisines, they will tell you (along with French and Chinese), and a revelation to most Americans in its healthful and delicious use of vegetables, yogurt, and whole grains. The small restaurants are so good and so extremely cheap that it really doesn't make sense to cook much except for breakfast and picnics.

Shop Patterns

Groceries are sold only in small dark shops even in big city bazaars. Fruits and vegetables can be bought from farmers in small towns on market day or by the roadside in the country. All prices in Turkey can be haggled, but unlike friends who enjoy this sport, we opt out and just pay what's asked. Some shops specialize in candy and pastries. A nice feature of Turkish shopping is that the seller will often insist on giving you a little something more free after you have made a purchase. Major souvenir shopping involves drinking tea with the proprietor, but this custom does not usually apply to food shopping.

What to Buy

If you're putting together a picnic, olives and cheese are good, as in Greece, and the bread is excellent in a sturdy sort of way. In late summer, melons and sweet red peppers are particularly delicious. Although Turkey is a Moslem country, beer is readily available, Efes Pils or Turkish Tuborg, but wine is not so common. If you have a sweet tooth, you'll want to try Turkish Delight and other sticky goodies in the candy shops. Again as in Greece, coffee is powder or Nescafe. Tea, however, is excellent, and comes in interesting flavor variations like apple or cinnamon.

Closing Hours

The national art in Turkey is small business, and they never close while there is a chance of customers.

Eating Out

It is a strange but easily verifiable fact in Turkey that the quality of the meal is in inverse relationship to the size of the check. The little outdoor joints up the hill by the bus station (or "santral garaji") where you can eat for a dollar, will serve better food than the big glossy restaurants with harbor views. Pideci shops sell big rounds of fresh hot flat bread topped with vegetables, eggs, or meat (probably the ancestor of pizza). In a lokanta, or cafe, the waiter will escort you to two big display cases (one hot, one cold) where you can point to your dinner. But be aware that Turks think of menus in terms of a cold mezze (or spread of dishes) followed by a hot mezze.

Menus

Turkish Breakfast

One of the daily pleasures of traveling in Turkey is the distinctive national breakfast. It is usually served outdoors, on wobbly little tables, and the menu is always the same. The fun is the contrasts of the flavors and making it all come out even at the end. An inevitable part of Turkish breakfast is the bee that zooms in to sit on the edge of the jam and then tumbles in, kicking his heels and buzzing in abandoned ecstasy.

- A big basket of hunks of fresh bread
- Butter and jam
- Feta cheese and one other hard cheese like Kaseri
- Black olives
- Tomato slices
- A bottomless pot of tea

Bursa Kebab in Galipoli

In this small harbor town famous for a World War I battle, we wandered into a tiny restaurant drawn by the mouth-watering fragrance from the lamb roasting on a spit in the window. I forget what we ordered, but they took pity on our ignorance and brought us bursa kebab instead, crackling and savory, topped with foaming brown butter which the waiter poured from a little copper pot with great ceremony. Afterward the waiter's assistant brought fresh napkins, sprayed our hands with perfumed water, and then plunked down a mason jar in which swam two exquisite Siamese fighting fish, one red, one blue. After a few minutes we figured out that the intention was for us to enjoy watching them while we had our coffee. The spirit was fed as well as the body.

- Bursa kebab (a plate-sized round of hot pide bread laid thickly over with tiny crisp slices of grilled lamb, a sparse layer of tomato sauce, and a generous drizzle of brown butter)
- Yogurt ringed with tomato slices
- Turkish coffee

CZECH REPUBLIC

The Czech people and Czech cooking are among the great and delightful surprises of rediscovering Eastern Europe. Both have a Germanic sensibleness lightened with a touch of whimsy and sweetness. Visiting the capital, Prague, is like being invited to a charming party. Although flooded with tourists, the city accepts her guests like a gracious hostess concerned that every one have a good time. The Baroque and Art Nouveau buildings, the wide squares full of street life, the serene Moldau crossed by picturesque bridges, the cheap and excellent small restaurants and cafes, the lively and inexpensive theater and concert scene—all make Prague very special. In the countryside there are cool forests to the north and unspoiled walled medieval towns to the south. (Don't miss Cesky Krumlov—it's a gem.)

Shop Patterns

The kind of Czech shops we love best are the cukrarnas—coffee-and-pastry places where you can stuff yourself from a dizzying assortment of whipped cream cake and custard goodies for less than a dollar. We recommend the one in Prague at the Hotel Julius on Vaclav Namesti, opposite MacDonalds. Ordinary edibles like cheese, yogurt, cold cuts, wine and beer are sold in small delicatessens called "potraviny." Cleaning products and paper goods are found in a separate kind of store. Fruits and vegetables are sold from stands on the street. Occasionally outside the cities you can find small super-markets, which are often German chains like Spar. In Prague the Krone Department Store on Vaclav Street has a cafeteria counter with delicious and very reasonably priced hot food for take-out: roast duck, chicken, and pork, goulash, noodles and vegetables.

What to Buy

Take-out pastries and roast duck, obviously. But also excellent are thinly sliced Prague ham and the breads and rolls, especially the salt twists.

As for drinkables, Pilsner Urquell is reputed to be the best beer in the world. Budvar is the antecedent of our Budweiser, but infinitely better. We were so busy comparing them that we didn't even try the wine.

There are still a few gaps in the food distribution system left over from communism. The most obvious is the scarcity of fresh meat, and of butchers who know how to cut it. Asking for decaf coffee will only get you puzzled shrugs; it hasn't been so long since Czechs couldn't get any coffee at all.

Closing Hours

Other than Sunday closing, the shops keep quite reasonable hours—open throughout the day until sixish.

Eating Out

The small restaurants are cheap and pleasant, so this is another country where you won't want to cook every night. Most menus are in Czech, German, and sort of

English and the waiters are kind and helpful. The food tends to be slow-cooked meat and poultry with gravy and noodles or dumplings—heavy but savory. The goulash is better than in Hungary, so eat it here. Don't expect much salad. For lunch "buffets" serve huge ready-made sandwiches and pastries, and the world's best bratwurst is sold from stands on Vaclav Street for sixty cents.

Menu

After a lovely day wandering the beautiful streets of Prague, we picked up the crispy roast duck at the take-out counter at Krone Department Store, hopped on the tram, and were home to our backyard campground in minutes. There we sat out under the apple trees and drank our beer while the soup simmered.

- Pilsner Urquell
- Potato soup with dill
- Half a roast duck
- Applesauce (from the campground apples)
- Salt twists
- Sliced cucumbers
- Whipped cream cake

HUNGARY

Gypsy music, wild horseback riding shows, and colorful peasant crafts are some of the pleasures of the land of the Magyars that make up for this country's flat, uninteresting terrain. The tourist bureau, IBUSZ, has piles of gorgeous full-color brochures, but the folks there are not otherwise very kindly. The food is spicy with the ubiquitous paprika, rich with sour cream, and leans heavily on noodles to hold up the meat and sauce, and the pastry shops are even better than in the Czech

Republic. Plan to gain weight. Food stores are easy to find and well-stocked—and in Budapest many stay open all night!

Shop Patterns

Everywhere you look there are small government-sponsored supermarkets called ABCs. They sell all the usual staples plus good fresh bread. Open-air markets are huge and bountiful in Budapest; two of the best are Skala Csarnok (two blocks south of Blaha Lujza Square) and Feny Utca (one block north of Moszkva Square). The Central Market is near Kalvin ter metro. Sidewalk food vendors are on nearly every corner in the city, and even the metro stations have excellent bakeries. Cukraszda display a mouth-watering selection of gorgeous pastries.

What to Buy

Hungarian sausage, which you will see festooned behind the counter, is excellent. Try also the small round yellow pickled peppers. Whole fried carp can be bought at stands in the Budapest open-air markets or at Lake Balaton—eat it with your fingers right there or take it home for a sensible meal with salad or vegetables. In late summer and fall the markets blaze with heaps of scarlet sweet peppers.

Wines are superb, especially Egri Bikaver, a smooth gutsy red called "Bull's Blood." Lake Balaton Riesling, at ninety cents a bottle, is light and sparkling. Tokaji Aszu is a dessert wine, rich and sweet.

Closing Hours

This country is an exception to the general need to be alert about shopping times in Europe. The Hungarian version of the mini-mart is called a "non-stop," and they stay open 24 hours a day.

Eating Out

Restaurants are cheap and pretty good. Try, of course, the gulyas—a beef and potato stew in paprika sauce known to us as goulash. But it is even more fun to satisfy those hunger pangs by browsing on the interesting street food: "langos," a puffy deep-fried potato pancake with sour cream or cheese, or waffles from a "goffri" stand. And afterwards there are always the cukraszda, where you should not miss the dobos tort with its layers of cake and whipped cream topped with hard carmel.

Menu

One rainy October we found to our joy that although most of Lake Balaton was closed, the Bergmann Konditorei in Balatonfuhred on Route 71 was still creating their exquisite pastries. We brought some home carefully and built dinner around them while we listened to gypsy music on the radio.

- Egri Bikaver
- Red and yellow peppers, onion, and garlic stewed with rounds of spicy Hungarian sausage
- Chunks of fresh bread to sop up the sauce
- Dobos tort

TRIP LOG
To Remember The Good Times . . .

Use the journal forms in this section (make as many copies as you need—one for each day) to record the practical information and the memorable events of your trip. This will provide a useful and enjoyable memento that will help you relive your European adventure for years to come. And it will give you something to do in the campground after dinner.

DAILY TRIP LOG

TRIP DAY:_____DATE_____
FROM:_____ ODO:_____
TO:_____ODO:_____
WEATHER:_____KM TRAVELED:_____
PHOTOS TAKEN:_____EXPENSES:_____
_____Fuel:_____
_____Camp:_____
_____Groceries:_____
_____Restaurant:_____
_____Misc.Fees:_____
                TOTAL EXPENSES:_____

HIGHLIGHTS & OBSERVATIONS:

_____

_____

_____

_____

_____

_____

_____

_____

Index

AA Camping and Caravanning in Europe, 105
Agencies, rental. See Rental agencies for vans and motor-homes
Agencies, sales. See Dealers
Agencies, shipping. See Shipping vans and motorhomes
Air flights, 67
Alcohol while driving, 102, 221
Amsterdam as a place to buy a van or motorhome, 33-34, 38-41,
APK sticker, 41
Aussie-Kiwi Van Mart, 45
Austria
    auto club, 91
    borders, 84
    freecamping, 126
    highway laws, 99
    roads, 79
Autobahn, 77-78, 122
Automobile associations, 90-93, 95, 105, 108, 111, 115
Bathing. See Showers
Bedding, 31, 73
Beds, van and motorhome, 52
    See also Interiors, van and motorhome
Beer, 142-143, 187, 201, 213, 217, 220-221, 226, 229
Belgium
    auto club, 91
    highway laws, 99
Booking a van or motorhome, 19-21
Borders, international, 82-84, 98
Brakes, van and motorhome, 54

Breakdowns, 90-93
Breakfasts, international, 177
Britain. See Great Britain.
Bulgaria
    auto club, 91
    camping, 117
    highway laws, 100
Buy-back guarantee, 13, 17, 33-35, 62
Buying a van or motorhome
    new, 57-61
    used, 31-57
Campgrounds, 13, 103-118, 131, 159
    and children, 153
    directories, 105-106, 111-112, 115
    Croatia, 118
    Czech Republic, 117
    France, 115, 117
        Paris, 112-113
    Germany
        Munich, 113-114
    Great Britain, 115
        London, 111-112
    Greece, 116-117
    Hungary, 117, 118
    Italy
        Venice, 118
    Netherlands, 114
    Portugal, 106, 116
    Spain, 115-116
    Turkey, 118
Camping, 103-126
Camping and Caravanning in France, Michelin, 115
Camping Carnet, 68, 106, 111

"Camping Gaz," 172-173

The Caravan Club, Great Britain, 111, 115

Certified Locations, 115

Cheap Eats in Paris, 195

Cheese, 193, 200, 204, 208, 213, 223

Chez Campanile, 195

Children, 149-158
    sights with "kid appeal," 154-158

"The Chunnel," 97

Closing times, 107-108, 183-184, 188, 194-195, 201, 205, 209, 213, 218, 223, 226, 229, 231

Clothing optional campgrounds, 109-110, 118

Clutch, 54-55

Coffee, 142-144, 205, 207, 229

Commonwealth of Independent States, 99

Cooking, 171-178
    equipment, 31, 174-175

Cost
    of buying a van or motorhome, 33-35, 57, 59, 148
    of campgrounds, 106
    of gasoline, 89-90
    of renting a van or motorhome, 29, 38, 148
    of shipping a van or motorhome, 60-61
    total, 148
    See also Money

Credit cards, 67, 69, 73, 78, 80, 83, 90, 146-147, 182

Croatia
    campground, 118
    highway laws, 100

Crystal Palace Caravan Harbour, 111-112, 188

Currency. See Money

Czech Republic
    auto club, 91
    campgrounds, 117, 118
    food shopping, 228-230
    highway laws, 100
    language, 141
    menu, 230
    roads, 80

Dealers, van and motorhome, 18-25, 33-35, 57-59
    Amsterdam, 38-39
    Frankfurt, 49
    London, 43-45

Denmark
    auto club, 91
    food shopping, 220-221
    highway laws, 100
    language, 139

Diesel fuel, 62, 90

Dishes. See Cooking, equipment

Doctors, 161

Dogs, 149-150

"The Dragon," 131

Driving, 75-102
    in cities, 86-87

Dumpstations, 108

Eastern Europe
    borders, 84
    campgrounds, 117
    highway laws, 99-102

Emergency road serivce, 90-93, 99-102

Engines, van and motorhome, 54-57
    compression, 56-57

England. See Great Britain

English Channel, 97-98, 176

Europa Camping, 105-106, 111

The Eurotunnel, 97

Evaluating a van or motorhome, 51-57

Exercise, 160

Ferries, 30, 83, 97-99, 176

Finland
    auto club, 91

highway laws, 101
Fire safety, 162
Flights, airplane, 67
A *Food Lover's Guide to France*, 195
Food shopping, 179-186
Ford Transit, 30-34
Foreign Towing Handbook and Directory, 115
France
  auto club, 91
  campgrounds, 115, 117, 131-132
  food shopping, 189-197
  freecamping, 122, 125, 132
  highway laws, 100
  language, 139
  menus, 195-197
  motorhome rental agency, 23
  roads, 78, 122
Frankfurt as a place to buy a van or motorhome, 47-51
Freecamping, 53, 94, 118-126, 132
F(rei) K(orper) K(ultur), 109-110
Fusina Camping, Italy, 118
Gaaspar Camping, Netherlands, 114
Gas stations, 81, 88-90
Gasoline, 60-62, 88-90
Germany
  auto club, 92, 108
  campgrounds, 113-114, 117
  food shopping, 197-203
  freecamping, 119, 122, 125
  highway laws, 100
  language, 139-140, 141
  menus, 202-203
  motorhome rental agencies, 23-24, 49
  refundable export tax, 60-61
  roads, 77-78, 122
Great Britain
  auto club, 92, 105, 111, 115
  campgrounds, 111-112, 115

food shopping, 186-189
highway laws, 99-100
language, 138
menus, 189
motorhome rental agencies, 22-23, 41-45
roads, 79, 122
Greece
  auto club, 92
  borders, 84, 98
  campgrounds, 116
  freecamping, 116, 125
  highway laws, 101
  language, 140
  menus, 207
  motorhome rental agencies, 24
  roads, 80
Guidebooks, 95
Gypsies, 120
Health, 72, 159-169, 171
  insurance, 161
Heaters, van and motorhome, 31, 55
Highway laws. See Traffic laws and individual countries
Highway rest areas, 78, 81, 122, 133
Holland. See Netherlands
Homesickness, 166
Hours, closing. See Closing times
Housekeeping in a van or motorhome, 163-164
Hungary
  auto club, 92
  campgrounds, 118
  food shopping, 230-232
  highway laws, 101
  language, 141
  menus, 232
  roads, 80
Hypermarches, 90, 183, 190-193
Importing a van or motorhome, 17, 60

Insurance, health, 161
Insurance, marine, 60
Insurance, vehicle, 18, 29, 35, 59
    Amsterdam, 41
    Frankfurt, 50
    London, 47
Interiors, van and motorhome,26,
    28, 30, 31, 36-37, 40, 42, 44,
    52-53, 150, 164-166
International Camping Carnet,
    68, 111
International Driving Permit, 68
International Money Orders, 147
Italy
    auto club, 92
    campgrounds, Venice, 118
    food shopping, 207-210
    freecamping, 122
    highway laws, 101
    language, 140
    menus, 209-210
    motorhome rental agencies,
    24-25
    roads, 78
Jet lag, 160-161
Kitchens, van and motorhome,
    53, 73, 162, 172-176
Kosmet
    highway laws, 100
Language, 116, 129-130, 135-144,
    181-182
Laundry, 107, 109
Leasing vans and motorhomes,
    18-31
Liechtenstein
    highway laws, 101
Linens, 31, 73
London
    as a place to buy a van or
    motorhome, 41-47
    campgrounds, 111-112
    freecamping, 119
London A to Z, 112

Luxembourg
    auto club, 92
    highway laws, 101
Macedonia
    borders, 84
    highway laws, 100
Maps, 95
Mechanical warranty, 35
Medicine, 161
Menus, 176-177
    Czech Republic, 230
    France, 195-197
    Germany 202-230
    Great Britain, 189
    Greece, 207
    Hungary, 232
    Italy, 209-210
    Netherlands, 214-215
    Portugal, 218-219
    Spain, 224-225
    Sweden, 221-222
    Turkey, 227-228
Michelin's *Camping and
    Caravanning in France,* 115
Money, 69, 83, 145-148, 182
Montenegro
    highway laws, 100
Mosquitoes, 121, 163
M.O.T. Certificate, 46
Motorhomes
    buying new, 57-61
    buying used, 31-57
    equipment, 31, 71-72, 107,
    151, 174-175
    evaluating, 51-57
    interiors, 36-37, 40, 42, 44,
    52-53, 150, 164-166
    leasing, 17-31
    renting, 17-31
    shipping, 17-18
    size, 29-31, 150
    types, 28-31, 36-37, 40, 42,
    44

Munich
  campgrounds, 113-114
  freecamping, 119
Navigator, 85
Netherlands
  auto club, 92
  campgrounds, 114
  food shopping, 210-215
  highway laws, 101
  language, 138
  menus, 214-215
  motorhome rental agencies,
    21-11, 39
No-parking signs, 94, 121
Norway
  auto club, 92
  food shopping, 219-221
  highway laws, 101
  language, 139
Nudist campgrounds, 109-110, 118,
  193
Outdoor markets, 180-182, 198,
  211, 216, 231
"P" sign, 81, 94, 122-123
Packing, 70-73
  children, 150-152
  cooking equipment, 174-175
Paris
  campgrounds, 112-113
  freecamping, 119
Parking signs, 81, 94
Passports, 54, 68, 84
Pedestrian safety, 161-162
Petrol, 60-62, 88-90
Phrasebooks, 136
"The Po," 127-128
Poland
  auto club, 92
  camping, 117
  highway laws, 102
Portugal
  auto club, 92
  borders, 84

  campgrounds, 106, 116
  food shopping, 215-219
  freecamping, 122-123, 125
  highway laws, 102
  language, 140
  menus, 218-219
  roads, 122-123
Prague, 228
  campgrounds, 117
Prescription drugs, 72, 161
Private sellers, 33
  Amsterdam, 40-41
  Frankfurt, 50
  London, 45-47
Propane, 53, 88-89, 172-173
Recycling, 109
Refrigerators, van and motorhome,
  31, 53, 173
Registration, vehicle, 18, 29, 35
  Amsterdam, 41
  Frankfurt, 50
  London, 47
Rental agencies, van and
  motorhome, 21-19
Renting vans and motorhomes, 18-
  31
Rest areas, highway, 78, 81, 122,
  132
Restaurants, 188, 195, 201-202,
  205, 206, 209, 214, 218,
  221, 226-227, 229-230, 232
Right-hand drive, 41-43, 79, 88,
  161-162
Roads, 74-81
  signs, 93-94, 121-122, 136
Romania
  auto club, 92
  camping, 117
  highway laws, 102
Roundabouts, 88
Rust, 52
Scandinavia
  food shopping, 219-222

language, 139
menus, 221-111
Seasons, 65-67
Seat belts, 99, 150-151
Security, 128, 167-169
Serbia
    highway laws, 100
Shipping vans and motorhomes
    agencies, 62-63
    from Europe, 17, 60
    to Europe, 17, 61-63
Shopping, food. See Food shopping
Showers, 30, 107, 131-133
Signs, road, 93-94, 121-122, 136
Sinks, van and motorhome, 31, 53,
    173-174
Slovenia
    highway laws, 100
Spain
    campgrounds, 115-116
    food shopping, 222-225
    freecamping, 123
    highway laws, 102
    language, 141
    menus, 224-225
    roads, 79, 80, 122-123
Specifications, new vehicle, U.S.
    and Canadian, 60
Speed limits, 76-77, 99-1102
"Squats," 130-131
Street signs. See Roads, signs
Storage in vans and motorhomes,
    53, 164, 170
Stoves, van and motorhome, 31, 53,
    162, 172-173
Supermarkets, 182-183, 192, 198,
    220, 229. See also
    Hypermarches
Sweden
    food shopping, 220-221
    freecamping, 125
    highway laws, 102
    language, 139

menus, 221-222
Switzerland
    auto club, 93
    food shopping, 192, 194
    menus, 197
    motorhome rental agencies, 25
    roads, 79
Take Your Kids to Europe, 153
Tapas, 223-224
Taxes, vehicle, 18, 29, 60-61
Telephones, 144
Thalkirchen Campground, 113-114
Toilets, 30, 107, 121, 127-131, 137,
    140, 150
Toll roads, 78-80, 122
Tourist bureaus, 86-87, 105, 230
Traffic laws, 77, 99-102
Transmission, 55
Travel agents, 19
Traveler's cheques, 106, 147, 169
"Travelling with Children" service,
    153
Trip Log, 234
Turkey
    auto club, 93
    borders, 84
    campgrounds, 118
    food shopping, 225-228
    highway laws, 102
    language, 141
    menus, 227-228
TUV sticker, 50-51
Unleaded fuel, 60-62
"The van choreography," 164-166
Vans
    buying new, 57-61
    buying used, 31-57
    equipment, 31, 71-72, 107, 151,
    174-175
    evaluating, 51-57
    interiors, 26, 28, 52-53, 150,
    164
    leasing, 17-31

renting, 17-31
shipping, 17-18, 60-63
size, 29-31, 150
types, 26, 28, 31, 33-34
Venice, campgrounds, 118
Visas, 68, 84
VW California, 28-29, 34
VW Joker, 26, 33, 34
VW Westfalia, 26, 33, 34, 57-58
Water, 159-160, 173
Weather, 65-67
Wine, 143, 193, 200-201, 205, 209,
217, 221, 223, 231